IMMIGRATION IN THE 21ST CENTURY: POLITICAL, SOCIAL AND ECONOMIC ISSUES



# THE U.S. ASYLUM SYSTEM

## TRENDS IN CLAIMS, FRAUD RISKS AND PREVENTION CONTROLS

# IMMIGRATION IN THE 21ST CENTURY: POLITICAL, SOCIAL AND ECONOMIC ISSUES

Additional books in this series can be found on Nova's website
under the Series tab.

Additional e-books in this series can be found on Nova's website
under the eBooks tab.

IMMIGRATION IN THE 21ST CENTURY: POLITICAL, SOCIAL AND ECONOMIC ISSUES

# THE U.S. ASYLUM SYSTEM

# TRENDS IN CLAIMS, FRAUD RISKS AND PREVENTION CONTROLS


EUGENE JAMES MARTIN
EDITOR



NOVINKA

*New York*

## NOTICE TO THE READER



**Library of Congress Cataloging-in-Publication Data**

ISBN: 978-1-63485-491-7

*Published by Nova Science Publishers, Inc. † New York*

# CONTENTS

# PREFACE

Each year, tens of thousands of aliens in the United States apply for asylum, which provides refuge to those who have been persecuted or fear persecution on protected grounds. Asylum officers in the Department of Homeland Security's (DHS) U.S. Citizenship and Immigration Services (USCIS) and immigration judges in the Department of Justice's (DOJ) Executive Office for Immigration Review (EOIR) adjudicate asylum applications. This book addresses what DHS and DOJ data indicate about trends in asylum claims; the extent to which DHS and DOJ have designed mechanisms to prevent and detect asylum fraud; and the extent to which DHS and DOJ designed and implemented processes to address any asylum fraud that has been identified.

In: The U.S. Asylum System
Editor: Eugene James Martin
ISBN: 978-1-63485-491-7


*Chapter 1*

# ASYLUM: ADDITIONAL ACTIONS NEEDED TO ASSESS AND ADDRESS FRAUD RISKS*

*United States Government Accountability Office*

## WHY GAO DID THIS STUDY

Each year, tens of thousands of aliens in the United States apply for asylum, which provides refuge to those who have been persecuted or fear persecution on protected grounds. Asylum officers in DHS's USCIS and immigration judges in DOJ's EOIR adjudicate asylum applications.

GAO was as ked to review the status of the asylum system. This report addresses (1) what DHS and DOJ data indicate about trends in asylum claims, (2) the extent to which DHS and DOJ have designed mechanisms to prevent and detect asylum fraud, and (3) the extent to which DHS and DOJ designed and implemented processes to address any asylum fraud that has been identified. GAO analyzed DHS and DOJ data on asylum applications for fiscal years 2010 through 2014, reviewed DHS and DOJ policies and procedures related to asylum fraud, and interviewed DHS and DOJ officials in Washington, D.C., Falls Church, VA, and in asylum offices and immigration courts across the country s elected on the basis of application data and other factors.

---

* This is an edited, reformatted and augmented version of the United States Government Accountability Office publication, GAO-16-50, dated December 2015.

## What GAO Recommends

GAO recommends that DHS and DOJ conduct regular fraud risk assessments and that DHS, among other things, implement tools for detecting fraud patterns , develop asylum-specific guidance for fraud detection roles and responsibilities, and implement timeliness goals for pending termination reviews. DHS and DOJ concurred with GAO's recommendations.

## What GAO Found

The total number of asylum applications, including both principal applicants and their eligible dependents, filed in fiscal year 2014 (108,152) is more than double the number filed in fiscal year 2010 (47,118). As of September 2015, the Department of Homeland Security's (DHS) U.S. Citizenship and Immigration Services (USCIS) has a backlog of 106,121 principal applicants, of which 64,254 have exceeded required time frames for adjudication. USCIS plans to hire additional staff to address the backlog.

USCIS and the Department of Justice's (DOJ) Executive Office for Immigration Review (EOIR) have limited capabilities to detect asylum fraud. First, while both USCIS and EOIR have mechanisms to investigate fraud in individual applications, neither agency has assessed fraud risks across the asylum process, in accordance with leading practices for managing fraud risks. Various cases of fraud illustrate risks that may affect the integrity of the asylum system. For example, an investigation in New York resulted in charges against 30 defendants as of March 2014 for their alleged participation in immigration fraud schemes; 829 applicants associated with the attorneys and preparers charged in the case received asylum from USCIS, and 3,709 received asylum from EOIR. Without regular assessments of fraud risks, USCIS and EOIR lack reasonable assurance that they have implemented controls to mitigate those risks. Second, USCIS's capability to identify patterns of fraud across asylum applications is hindered because USCIS relies on a paper-based system for asylum applications and does not electronically capture some key information that could be used to detect fraud, such as the applicant's written statement. Asylum officers and USCIS Fraud Detection and National Security (FDNS) Directorate immigration officers told GAO that they can identify potential fraud by analyzing trends across asylum applications; however, they must rely on labor-intensive methods to do so.

Identifying and implementing additional fraud detection tools could enable USCIS to detect fraud more effectively while using resources more efficiently. Third, FDNS has not established clear fraud detection responsibilities for its immigration officers in asylum offices; FDNS officers we spoke with at all eight asylum offices told GAO they have limited guidance with respect to fraud. FDNS standard operating procedures for fraud detection are intended to apply across USCIS, and therefore do not reflect the unique features of the asylum system. Developing asylum-specific guidance for fraud detection, in accordance with federal internal control standards, would better position FDNS officers to understand their roles and responsibilities in the asylum process.

To address identified instances of asylum fraud, USCIS can, in some cases, terminate an individual's asylum status. USCIS terminated the asylum status of 374 people from fiscal years 2010 through 2014 for fraud. In August 2015, USCIS adopted a target of 180 days for conducting initial reviews, in which the asylum office reviews evidence and decides whether to begin termination proceedings, when the asylee has applied for adjustment to lawful permanent resident status; however, this goal applies only to a subset of asylees and pertains to initial reviews. Further, asylees with pending termination reviews may be eligible to receive certain federal benefits. Developing timeliness goals for all pending termination reviews would help USCIS better identify the staffing resources needed to address the terminations workload.

## ABBREVIATIONS

| | |
|---|---|
| BFCA | Benefit Fraud and Compliance Assessment |
| BIA | Board of Immigration Appeals |
| DHS | Department of Homeland Security |
| DOJ | Department of Justice |
| EAD | Employment Authorization Document |
| EIC | Earned Income Credit |
| ELIS | Electronic Immigration System |
| EOIR | Executive Office for Immigration Review |
| FBI | Federal Bureau of Investigation |
| FDNS | Fraud Detection and National Security |
| FDNS-DS | FDNS Data System |
| HSI | Homeland Security Investigations |

| | |
|---|---|
| IBFA | Immigration Benefit Fraud Assessment |
| ICE | U.S. Immigration and Customs Enforcement |
| INA | Immigration and Nationality Act |
| INS | Immigration and Naturalization Service |
| LPR | lawful permanent resident |
| OPLA | Office of the Principal Legal Advisor |
| RAIO | Refugee, Asylum, and International Operations Directorate |
| RAPS | Refugee, Asylum, and Parole System |
| TOPS | Table of Organization Position System |
| USCIS | U.S. Citizenship and Immigration Services |

***

December 2, 2015

Congressional Requesters

U.S. immigration law provides that aliens within the United States may be granted humanitarian protection, in the form of asylum, if they demonstrate that they are unable or unwilling to return to their home country because of past persecution or a well-founded fear of future persecution based on their race, religion, nationality, membership in a particular social group, or political opinion. [1] According to the Office of the United Nations High Commissioner for Refugees, because of the experience of seeking asylum, and the often traumatic events precipitating an individual's flight from his or her home country, asylum seekers may experience psychological illness; trauma; depression; anxiety; aggression; and other physical, psychological, and emotional consequences.[2] Asylum decisions can have serious consequences. Granting asylum to an applicant with a genuine claim protects the asylee from being returned to a country where he or she has been or could in the future be persecuted.[3] On the other hand, granting asylum to an individual with a fraudulent claim jeopardizes the integrity of the asylum system by enabling the individual to remain in the United States, apply for certain federal benefits, and pursue a path to citizenship.[4] Given the potential consequences of asylum decisions, it is important that the asylum system is not misused. This protects the integrity of the legal immigration process and avoids the potentially serious consequences that could result if an applicant is wrongfully returned to his or her country of persecution or if an applicant whose asylum claim is fraudulent or who poses a threat to the United States is permitted to stay.

The Department of Homeland Security (DHS) and the Department of Justice (DOJ) share responsibility for the U.S. asylum system. Specifically, asylum officers within DHS's U.S. Citizenship and Immigration Services (USCIS) adjudicate affirmative applications—that is, claims filed with USCIS at the initiative of the alien. [5] An affirmative asylum applicant may be in the United States lawfully or unlawfully, and must file for asylum directly with USCIS within 1 year of his or her most recent arrival in the country unless he or she can demonstrate changed or extraordinary circumstances.[6] Within USCIS, the Fraud Detection and National Security Directorate (FDNS) is responsible for determining whether individuals filing for asylum pose a threat to national security or public safety or are engaging in asylum fraud. If USCIS determines that the applicant is ineligible for asylum and does not otherwise have lawful immigration status in the United States, asylum officers are to issue a Notice to Appear before DOJ's Executive Office for Immigration Review (EOIR) for adjudication in removal proceedings.[7] EOIR's immigration judges adjudicate both affirmative asylum claims referred by USCIS and defensive applications for asylum, which are asylum claims first made during removal proceedings as a defense against removal from the United States.[8] DHS's U.S. Immigration and Customs Enforcement's (ICE) Office of the Principal Legal Advisor (OPLA) trial attorneys are responsible for representing the U.S. government in immigration court proceedings, including asylum hearings, before EOIR. ICE's Homeland Security Investigations (HSI) is responsible for conducting criminal investigations regarding immigration-related document and benefit fraud, including asylum fraud referred by USCIS, OPLA, and EOIR.

The nature of the asylum system puts asylum officers and immigration judges in the position of adjudicating or ruling on asylum applications with what may be imperfect information. Specifically, U.S. asylum law states that testimonial information alone, without corroboration, may be sufficient for asylum applicants to meet the burden of proof for establishing asylum eligibility.[9] In part, this is because applicants may not be able to present documents, such as passports or birth certificates, if they fled their countries of persecution without them; may have come from countries where documentary evidence was not available; or may have fled with fraudulent documents to hide their true identity or to otherwise facilitate escape from harm. As such, asylum officers and immigration judges must make decisions, at times, with little or no documentation to support or refute an applicant's claim. These factors create a challenging environment in which adjudicators must attempt to reach the best decisions they can with the information available.

In 2008, we reported on USCIS's asylum adjudication process.[10] Among other things, we found that USCIS had designed quality assurance mechanisms to help ensure the integrity of asylum adjudications, but that some of the mechanisms could be improved. For example, we found that USCIS did not consistently solicit asylum officers' input on their training needs, local quality assurance reviews did not consistently take place in some asylum offices, and time constraints affected asylum officers' adjudications. We recommended that USCIS, among other things, solicit information from officers on their training needs, develop a plan to implement local quality reviews in all offices, and determine how much time is needed to adjudicate an asylum claim in a manner consistent with procedures and training. USCIS concurred and took action to implement these recommendations, such as implementing a training needs assessment, developing and implementing a program to review a sample of asylum officers' decisions in all offices, and revising asylum officers' performance measures to focus on quality rather than productivity standards.

The report of the Senate Appropriations Committee accompanying the DHS Appropriations Act, 2015, included a provision, and Congress requested, that we review the status of the asylum system.[11] This report (1) describes what DHS and DOJ data indicate about trends in the characteristics of asylum claims, (2) evaluates the extent to which DHS and DOJ have designed mechanisms to prevent and detect fraud in the asylum system, and (3) evaluates the extent to which DHS and DOJ have designed and implemented processes to address any fraud that has been identified in the asylum system.

To describe trends in the characteristics of asylum claims, we analyzed summary and record-level data from USCIS's Refugee, Asylum, and Parole System (RAPS) on asylum applications, adjudications, and grants by asylum offices nationwide for fiscal years 2010 through 2014.[12] To assess the reliability of the RAPS data, we reviewed USCIS documents about the design of RAPS, completed data entry and duplicate record checks, and discussed the reliability of the data with USCIS officials. We also analyzed two reports issued by EOIR's Office of Planning, Analysis, and Statistics from fiscal years 2010 through 2014—Asylum Statistics and Statistics Yearbook. These reports contain data about the characteristics of asylum applications adjudicated through the immigration courts in the period of our analysis.[13] To assess the reliability of the data in EOIR's reports, we reviewed documentation on EOIR's case management system and spoke with officials about how EOIR collects and monitors data. In fiscal year 2013, EOIR changed the methodology it used to compile its statistics in the reports; thus, data from previous fiscal year reports are not comparable with those reported in fiscal years 2013 and 2014 reports. As a result, we relied on the fiscal years 2013 and 2014 reports for our analyses. We determined that the USCIS and EOIR data about the characteristics of asylum claims were sufficiently reliable for our purposes.

To evaluate the extent to which DHS and DOJ have mechanisms in place to prevent and detect fraud in the asylum system, we compared USCIS and EOIR's asylum-related policies and procedures with, among other things, standards in *Standards for Internal Control in the Federal Government* and leading practices in GAO's *Framework for Managing Fraud Risk s in Federal Programs* (the Fraud Framework).[14] Regarding USCIS, we reviewed USCIS Asylum Division's *Affirmative Asylum Procedures Manual,* FDNS's *Fraud Detection Standard Operating Procedures,* and other USCIS policy documents. We reviewed past USCIS efforts to examine fraud in the USCIS asylum system and spoke with USCIS Office of Policy and Strategy officials who manage these efforts. We analyzed data from FDNS's case management system about the number of benefit fraud cases associated with asylum applications that were opened from fiscal year 2010 through 2014 and the number of those cases in which FDNS found fraud. To assess the reliability of these data, we reviewed policies about how data are entered into the system and interviewed FDNS immigration officers and headquarters officials and observed FDNS immigration officers using the system. We discuss our findings about the reliability of these data later in this report. In addition, we reviewed Asylum Division workforce planning efforts against principles in *Key Principles for Effective Strategic Workforce Planning* and interviewed Asylum Division officials about attrition among asylum officers.[15] We reviewed asylum officer attrition data from fiscal year 2010 through 2014, which USCIS compiled manually at our request. We discuss our findings about the reliability of these data later in this report. We also reviewed USCIS quality assurance policy documents and spoke with Asylum Division and Refugee, Asylum, and International Operations Directorate (RAIO) officials about quality assurance mechanisms in the asylum program. Furthermore, we analyzed USCIS asylum officer basic training materials, as well as training materials for FDNS immigration officers, and interviewed Asylum Division and RAIO headquarters officials about how asylum officers are trained to detect and prevent fraud. In particular, we reviewed USCIS Asylum Division quarterly training reports for fiscal year 2014 to analyze the weekly training activities in each asylum office for each week of the reporting quarter. We compared RAIO and Asylum Division training materials with material in

GAO's *Guide for Assessing Strategic Training and Development Efforts in the Federal Government*.[16]

To further evaluate the extent to which DHS and DOJ have designed mechanisms to prevent and detect asylum fraud, we visited five of the eight asylum offices—Newark, New Jersey; New York, New York; Los Angeles, California; Houston, Texas; and Arlington, Virginia. We selected these offices for site visits based on a variety of factors, including their number of asylum officers, the number of asylum applications they receive, and geographic proximity to EOIR immigration courts. During our site visits, we also visited immigration courts in New York, Los Angeles, Houston, and Arlington and observed asylum hearings in New York, Los Angeles, Houston, and Arlington. In addition, we interviewed approximately 11 ICE OPLA attorneys and 10 ICE HSI investigators in the New York, Los Angeles, Houston, and Arlington offices. In each asylum office, we observed asylum interviews and spoke with supervisory asylum officers, asylum officers, training officers, and FDNS immigration officers to obtain their perspectives on asylum fraud and the associated risks. We also conducted telephone interviews with asylum officers, training officers, and FDNS immigration officers in the remaining three asylum offices—Miami, Chicago, and San Francisco. Across the eight asylum offices, we spoke with 35 supervisory asylum officers, 37 asylum officers, 24 FDNS immigration officers (including four supervisors), and 12 training officers.[17] We spoke with supervisory asylum officers, asylum officers, and FDNS immigration officers in all eight asylum offices about the tools and systems that they use to identify and detect asylum fraud and the roles of asylum officers and FDNS immigration officers in asylum fraud detection. We also spoke with training officers in each of the eight asylum offices about how they develop and present training. Although the results of our visits and telephone interviews cannot be generalized to officers in all asylum offices or to all immigration courts, they provided first-hand observations on asylum adjudication practices and insights regarding policies and procedures to detect asylum fraud.

Regarding EOIR, we reviewed EOIR's Fraud and Abuse Prevention Program guidance and policy documentation, including the regulation that established EOIR's antifraud officer position. We also reviewed the *Immigration Judge Benchbook*, which includes tools, templates, and legal resources for immigration judges to use in their adjudications. We analyzed EOIR's fraud-related training materials for immigration judges and spoke with the antifraud officer about the fraud detection and prevention activities associated with this role. In addition, we analyzed EOIR Fraud Abuse

Prevention Program case files to determine the number of complaints received, number of case files opened, and number of asylum-related case files opened from fiscal year 2010 through fiscal year 2014 to evaluate their fraud detection activities. We also reviewed 35 EOIR Fraud Abuse Prevention Program case files, which EOIR identified as being all cases associated with asylum fraud.[18] While observing immigration court proceedings in New York City, Houston, and Arlington, including asylum cases, we spoke with court administrators and immigration judges about asylum fraud.

To evaluate the extent to which DHS and DOJ have designed and implemented processes to address any fraud that has been identified in the asylum system, we analyzed ICE HSI data on the number of asylum fraud-related indictments, criminal arrests, convictions, and administrative arrests as well as the number of asylum fraud cases initiated by HSI from fiscal year 2010 through fiscal year 2014. We also analyzed USCIS RAPS data to identify the number of individuals who have had their asylum status terminated because of fraud during this time period and any trends in asylum terminations because of fraud over those years. We used ICE Enforcement and Removal Operations data to analyze the outcomes for individuals whose asylum status was terminated for fraud from fiscal years 2010 through 2014. We assessed the reliability of these data by reviewing documentation about how data were collected; interviewing knowledgeable agency officials about the data; and conducting electronic testing for missing data, outliers, and obvious errors. We determined that these data were sufficiently reliable for the purposes of analyzing the number of asylum terminations because of fraud and the outcome of those terminations. We reviewed USCIS policy documents related to asylum terminations, as well as certain U.S. Circuit Court of Appeals decisions that were identified by Asylum Division officials as influencing how USCIS pursues asylum terminations because of fraud. We interviewed officials at five HSI locations—New York, New York; Washington, D.C.; Houston, Texas; Los Angeles, California; and Fairfax, Virginia— about how they receive asylum fraud referrals and how they investigate allegations of asylum fraud. We also interviewed EOIR officials about mechanisms to address identified asylum fraud in the immigration courts and how those mechanisms are used. We interviewed officials in the eight USCIS asylum offices, as well as Asylum Division officials, to determine how USCIS handles cases with identified fraud, including cases in which fraud is identified after asylum has been granted, and how USCIS tracks, monitors, and adjudicates cases in which an individual's asylum status is pending termination for identified fraud. We compared USCIS and EOIR mechanisms to address identified asylum fraud and the frequency of their use with our Fraud Framework to assess their likely effectiveness as a fraud deterrent.[19]

We conducted this performance audit from September 2014 to November 2015 in accordance with generally accepted government auditing standards. Those standards require that we plan and perform the audit to obtain sufficient, appropriate evidence to provide a reasonable basis for our findings and conclusions based on our audit objectives. We believe that the evidence obtained provides a reasonable basis for our findings and conclusions based on our audit objectives. We believe that the evidence obtained provides a reasonable basis for our findings and conclusions based on our audit objectives. Appendix I provides additional information on our scope and methodology.

# BACKGROUND

## Asylum Eligibility Requirements

To adjudicate asylum claims, USCIS asylum officers and EOIR immigration judges determine an applicant's eligibility for asylum by assessing whether the applicant has credibly established that he or she is a refugee within the meaning of section 101(a)(42)(A) of the Immigration and Nationality Act (INA), as amended. An applicant is eligible for asylum if he or she (1) applies from within the United States; (2) suffered past persecution, or has a well-founded fear of future persecution, based on race, religion, nationality, membership in a particular social group, or political opinion; and (3) is not statutorily barred from applying for or being granted asylum.[20] Among other things, the REAL ID Act of 2005 was a legislative effort to provide consistent standards for adjudicating asylum applications and to limit fraud.[21] Consistent with the REAL ID Act, the burden is on the applicant to establish past persecution or a well-founded fear of persecution, and asylum officers and immigration judges have the discretion to require documentary support for asylum claims.[22] To determine whether an applicant is credible, the act requires that asylum officers and immigration judges consider the totality of the applicant's circumstances and all relevant factors and states that a determination of the applicant's credibility may be based on any relevant factor.[23] Such factors could include, among others, the applicant's demeanor, candor, or responsiveness in the asylum interview or immigration court hearing, or any inaccuracies or falsehoods discovered in the applicant's written or oral statements, whether or not an inconsistency, inaccuracy, or falsehood goes to the heart of the applicant's claim.[24] However, an asylum officer or immigration judge may determine that an applicant is credible, considering the totality of the circumstances, even if there are inaccuracies, contradictions, or evidence of potential fraud. For example, an applicant may have lied to a U.S. consular officer in order to obtain a visa to travel to the United States when fleeing his or her home country, and still have a credible asylum claim.

## Overview of the Affirmative and Defensive Asylum Application Processes

To apply for affirmative asylum, an applicant submits a Form I-589, *Application for Asylum and for Withholding of Removal*, to USCIS. An applicant may include his or her spouse and unmarried children under the age of 21 who are physically present in the United States as dependent asylum applicants.[25] The applicant mails paper copies of the application and supporting documentation to a USCIS Service Center, which verifies that the application is complete, creates a hard-copy file, and enters information about the applicant, including biographic information as well as attorney and preparer information submitted with the application, into RAPS.[26] Subsequently, using the applicant's biographic data, RAPS initiates automated checks against other U.S. government databases containing criminal history information, immigration violation records, and address information, among other things. RAPS also schedules an appointment to fingerprint and photograph the applicant. The Service Center sends the applicant file to one of USCIS's eight asylum offices based on the applicant's residential address and the asylum office then schedules the applicant's interview with an asylum officer. In adjudicating asylum applications, USCIS policy requires asylum officers to review the applicant's hard-copy file; research country of origin information; verify that an applicant has completed fingerprinting requirements; and document the results of background, identity, and security checks, some of which are repeated in the asylum office to identify any relevant information that may have changed after the initial automated checks. Asylum officers are to use the information obtained through this process to (1) determine who is included in the application; (2) confirm the applicant's immigration status, asylum filing date, and date, place, and manner of entry into the United States; (3) become familiar with the asylum claim and the applicant's background and supporting documentation; (4) identify issues that could affect eligibility, such as criminal history, national security concerns, participation in human rights abuses, or adverse credibility or fraud indicators; and (5) identify issues that must be discussed in an interview with the applicant to determine asylum eligibility.[27]

During the interview, which is to be conducted in a nonadversarial manner, the asylum officer asks questions to assess the applicant's eligibility for asylum and determine whether his or her claim is credible.[28] If the asylum officer identifies inaccuracies, inconsistencies, or fraud in the asylum application, the applicant must be given an opportunity to explain such issues during the interview, according to the USCIS *Affirmative Asylum Procedures Manual*. An independent interpreter monitor listens to each affirmative asylum interview to ensure that the applicant's interpreter is correctly interpreting and to notify the interviewing officer of any discrepancies in interpretation. After the interview, the asylum officer considers the totality of the circumstances surrounding the applicant's claim and prepares a written decision. The decision is reviewed by a supervisor, who is to check for quality, accuracy, and legal sufficiency. After a supervisor has concurred with the decision, the decision notice is delivered in hard copy to the applicant.

If USCIS grants asylum to the applicant, the asylee is eligible to apply for adjustment to lawful permanent resident (LPR) status after 1 year.[29] If USCIS does not grant asylum and the applicant is present in the United States lawfully through other means, USCIS is to issue a Notice of Intent to Deny stating the reason(s) for asylum ineligibility and provide an opportunity for the applicant to respond. Whether or not asylum is granted, the applicant can continue living in the United States under his or her otherwise valid status. If USCIS does not grant asylum and the applicant is present in the United States unlawfully, USCIS is to refer the application to EOIR, together with a Notice to Appear, which requires that the applicant appear before an EOIR immigration judge for adjudication of the asylum claim in removal proceedings. Figure 1 provides an overview of the USCIS affirmative asylum process.

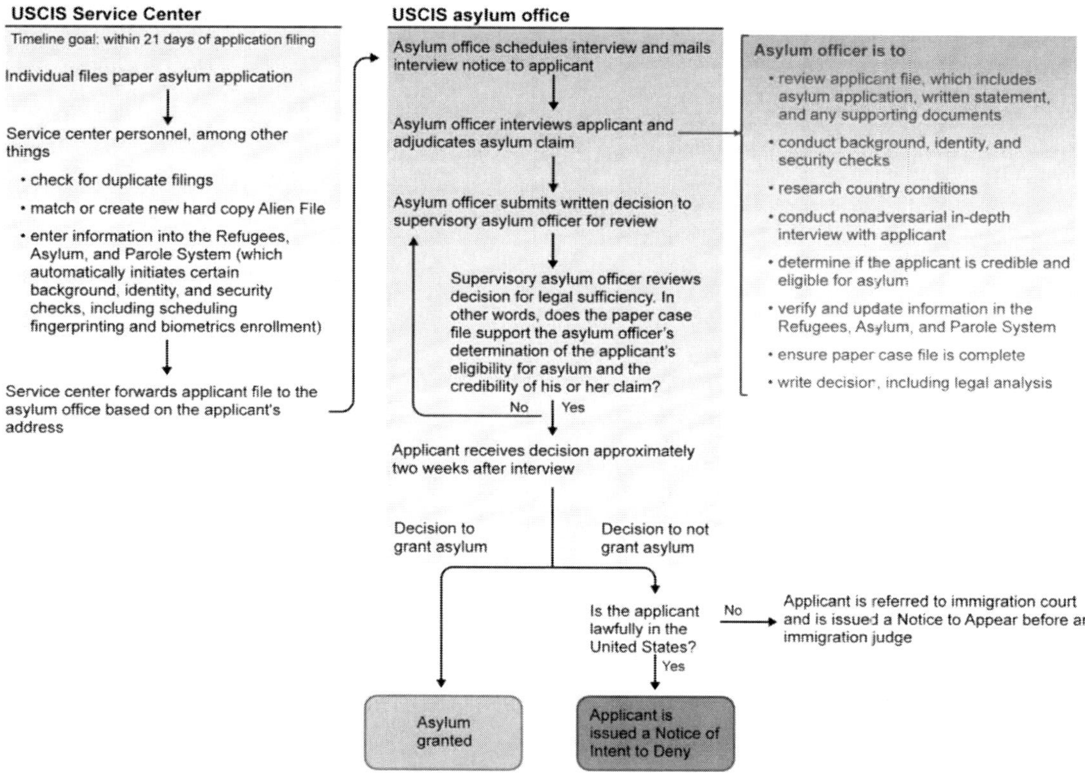


Source: GAO analysis of USCIS data.|GAO-16-50.

Figure 1. U.S. Citizenship and Immigration Services (USCIS) Affirmative Asylum Process.

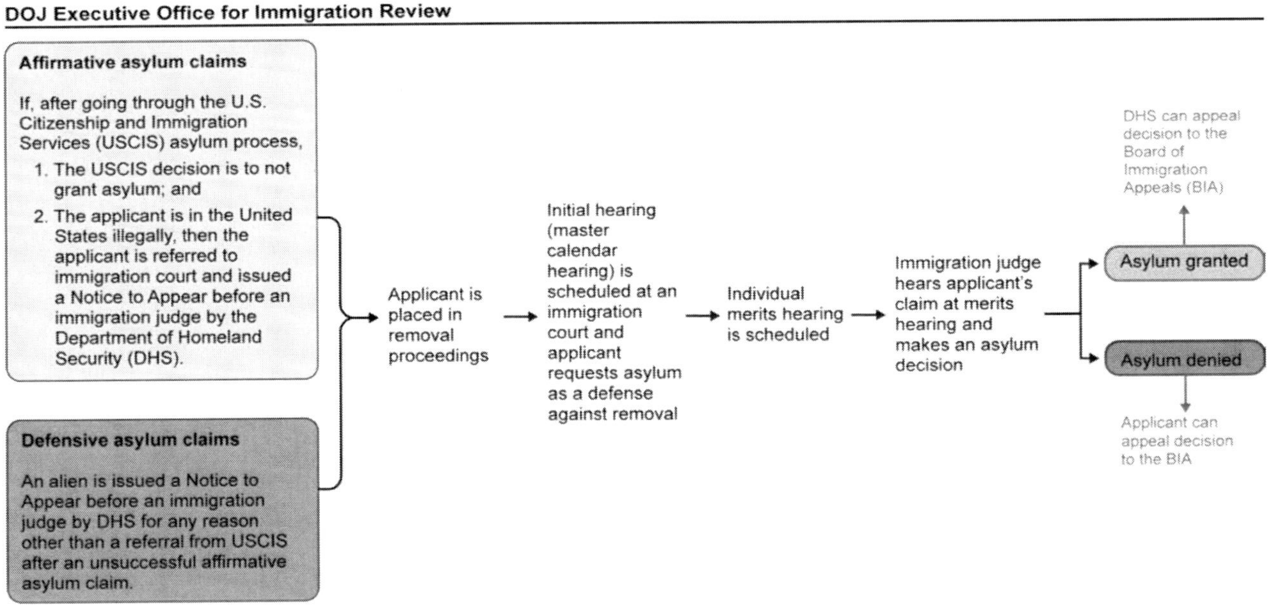

Source: GAO analysis of DOJ data.|GAO-16-50

Figure 2. Department of Justice (DOJ) Asylum Process.

EOIR follows the same procedures for defensive asylum applications and affirmative asylum referrals from USCIS. For affirmative asylum referrals, the immigration judge reviews the case *de novo*, meaning that the judge evaluates the applicant's affirmative asylum application anew and is not bound by an asylum officer's previous determination. EOIR asylum hearings are adversarial proceedings in which asylum applicants appear in removal proceedings for adjudication of the asylum claim, and may apply for other forms of relief or protection as a defense against removal from the United States. First, the judge conducts an initial hearing (referred to as a master calendar hearing) to, among other things, ensure that the applicant understands the court proceedings and schedule a hearing to specifically address the asylum application (referred to as a merits hearing).[30] Second, during the merits hearing, the judge hears testimony from the applicant and any other witnesses, oversees cross- examinations, and reviews evidence. ICE trial attorneys represent DHS in these proceedings. An asylum applicant may self-represent or may be represented by an attorney at no cost to the U.S. government. The judge may question the applicant or other witnesses. Judges render oral and, in some cases, written decisions after the immigration court proceedings end. If the judge determines that the applicant is eligible for asylum, the asylee can remain in the United States indefinitely unless asylum status is subsequently terminated.[31] A grant of asylum from an immigration judge confers the same benefits as a grant of asylum from a USCIS asylum officer. If the judge determines that the applicant is ineligible for asylum, and is removable, the judge may order the applicant to be removed from the United States, unless the applicant seeks (and receives) another form of relief from removal. Judges' decisions are final unless appealed to the Board of Immigration Appeals (BIA). Figure 2 provides an overview of the DOJ affirmative and defensive asylum process.

## Eligibility for Federal Benefits

Asylees, or individuals who have been granted asylum, are considered qualified aliens for the purpose of eligibility for federal, and state or local, public benefits.[32] Subject to certain statutory criteria, asylees may be eligible for a number of federal means-tested public benefits including Supplemental Security Income, Supplemental Nutrition Assistance Program, Temporary Assistance for Needy Families, and Medicaid.[33] In addition, asylees may also be eligible for federal student financial aid, among other benefits.[34] Asylees are authorized for employment in the United States as a result of their asylum status and can receive an Employment Authorization Document (EAD) issued by USCIS.[35] In addition, asylum applicants can receive an EAD after their applications have been pending, including in both the USCIS and EOIR adjudicative process, for 180 days, not including any delays requested or caused by the applicant such as requesting to reschedule or failing to appear at the asylum interview or, where applicable, the time between issuance of a request for evidence and receipt of the applicant's response.[36] Within 2 years of receiving asylum status, asylees can request derivative asylum status for their spouses and unmarried children under age 21, a provision that allows family members to join the asylee in the United States.[37]

## Fraud and Asylum

Immigration benefit fraud involves the willful misrepresentation of material fact for the purpose of obtaining an immigration benefit, such as asylum status, without lawful entitlement. Immigration benefit fraud is often facilitated by document fraud and identity fraud. Document fraud includes forging, counterfeiting, altering, or falsely making any document, or using, possessing, obtaining, accepting, or receiving such falsified documents in order to satisfy any requirement of, or to obtain a benefit under, the INA.[38] Identity fraud refers to the fraudulent use of others' valid documents. Fraud can occur in the affirmative and defensive asylum processes in a number of ways. For example, an applicant may file fraudulent supporting documents with his or her affirmative asylum application in an attempt to bolster the facts of a claim. Or, an applicant may submit a fraudulent address in order to file for asylum within the jurisdiction of an asylum office or immigration court perceived to be more likely to grant asylum than another office or court. Further, an attorney, preparer, or interpreter can, in exchange for fees from the applicant, prepare and file fraudulent documents, written statements, or supporting details about an applicant's asylum claim, with or without the applicant's knowledge or involvement. For the purposes of this report, we define asylum fraud as the willful misrepresentation of material fact(s), such as making false statements, submitting forged or falsified documents, or conspiring to do so, in support of an asylum claim.[39]

It is possible to terminate an individual's asylum status under certain circumstances, including where there is a showing of fraud in the application such that the individual was not eligible for asylum at the time it was granted.[40] By regulation, USCIS may only terminate asylum granted by USCIS; however, EOIR may terminate asylum granted by either USCIS or EOIR.[41] For cases granted by USCIS, except in the Ninth Circuit, USCIS issues the asylee a Notice of Intent to Terminate and conducts an interview in which the individual may present evidence of his or her asylum eligibility.[42] If termination is warranted, USCIS then provides written notice to the individual of termination of his or her asylum status and is to initiate removal proceedings for the individual in immigration court, as appropriate.[43] While in removal proceedings, the individual may reapply for asylum before an immigration judge.[44] The judge is not required to accept the determination of fraud made by USCIS and determines the respondent's eligibility for asylum anew.[45] For cases granted by an immigration judge, the BIA, or by USCIS in the Ninth Circuit, ICE OPLA may petition the immigration court to re-open a case in which an individual has been granted asylum and request the termination of the individual's asylum status because of fraud.[46] In such a case, ICE OPLA must prove, by a preponderance of evidence, that there was fraud in the asylum application that would have rendered the asylee ineligible for asylum at the time it was granted.[47] The immigration judge has jurisdiction to conduct an asylum termination hearing as part of the removal proceeding, and if asylum status is terminated, the individual may be subject to removal from the United States. [48]

## GAO's Fraud Framework

Our Fraud Framework is a comprehensive set of leading practices that serves as a guide for program managers to use when developing efforts to combat fraud in a strategic, risk-based manner.[49] The framework describes leading practices for establishing an organizational structure and culture that are conducive to fraud risk management, designing and implementing controls to prevent and detect potential fraud, and monitoring and evaluating to provide assurances to managers that they are effectively preventing, detecting, and responding to potential fraud. Managers may perceive a conflict between their priorities to fulfill the program's mission, such as efficiently disbursing funds or providing services to beneficiaries, and taking actions to safeguard taxpayer dollars from improper use. However, the purpose of proactively managing fraud risks is to facilitate, not hinder, the program's mission and strategic goals by ensuring that taxpayer dollars and government services serve their intended purposes. Figure 3 illustrates our Fraud Framework.

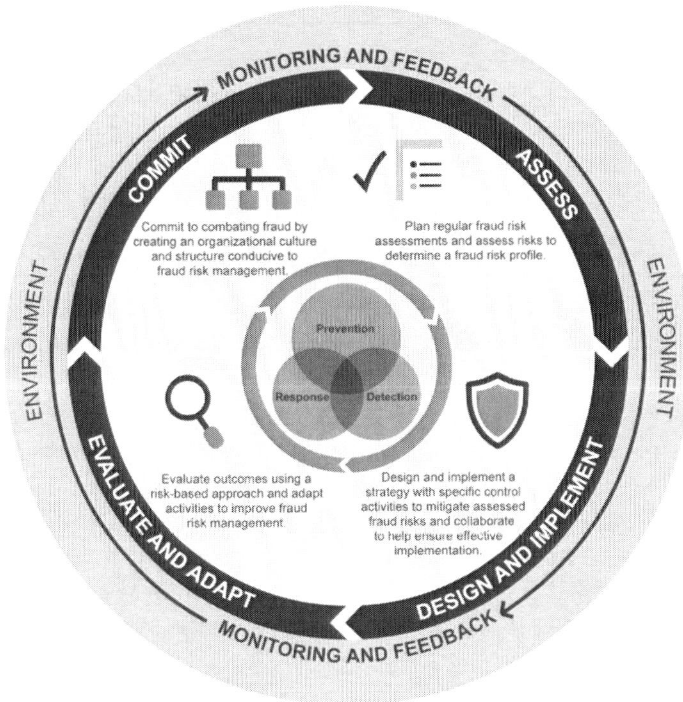


Source: GAO.|Gao-16-50.

Figure 3. GAO's Fraud Frame work.

The Fraud Framework includes control activities that help agencies prevent, detect, and respond to fraud risks as well as structures and environmental factors that influence or help managers achieve their objectives to mitigate fraud risks. The framework consists of four components for effectively managing fraud risks: commit, assess, design and implement, and evaluate and adapt. Leading practices for each of these components include the following:

- Commit: create an organizational culture to combat fraud at all levels of the agency, and designate an entity within the program office to lead fraud risk management activities;
- Assess: assess the likelihood and impact of fraud risks and determine risk tolerance and examine the suitability of existing controls and prioritize residual risks;
- Design and implement: develop, document, and communicate an antifraud strategy, focusing on preventive control activities; and

- Evaluate and adapt: collect and analyze data from reporting mechanisms and instances of detected fraud for real-time monitoring of fraud trends, and use the results of monitoring, evaluations, and investigations to improve fraud prevention, detection, and response.

## THE NUMBER OF ASYLUM APPLICATIONS FILED PER FISCAL YEAR HAS INCREASED EVERY YEAR FROM 2010 TO 2014

### The Number of Asylum Applications Filed in Fiscal Year 2014 Is More Than Double the Total Filed in Fiscal Year 2010

The total number of asylum applications (principal applicants and their eligible dependents), including affirmative and defensive applications, increased from 47,118 in fiscal year 2010 to 108,152 in fiscal year 2014, an increase of 130 percent. During this time, affirmative asylum applications filed directly with USCIS increased by a total of 131 percent.[50] Defensive asylum applications filed with EOIR increased 125 percent.[51] Table 1 shows the number of affirmative and defensive asylum applications filed each year for fiscal years 2010 through 2014.

**Table 1. Affirmative and Defensive Asylum Applications, Fiscal Years 2010 through 2014**

| Fiscal year | Affirmative applications | Defensive applications | Total applications filed |
|---|---|---|---|
| 2010 | 34,374 | 12,744 | 47,118 |
| 2011 | 43,148 | 17,861 | 61,009 |
| 2012 | 53,293 | 19,648 | 72,941 |
| 2013 | 60,076 | 22,535 | 82,611 |
| 2014 | 79,485 | 28,667 | 108,152 |
| Total | 270,376 | 101,455 | 371,831 |

Source: GAO analysis of U.S. Citizenship and Immigration Services (USCIS) and Executive Office for Immigration Review (EOIR) data. | GAO-16-50

Note: Defensive applications do not include applicants who applied affirmatively with USCIS and were referred to EOIR. Al so, according to USCIS officials, USCIS does not include dependents when counting affirmative asylum applications.

**Table 2. Principal and Dependent Affirmative Asylum Applications, Fiscal Years 2010 through 2014**

| Fiscal year | Dependent applications | Principal applications | Total affirmative applications filed |
|---|---|---|---|
| 2010 | 6,266 | 28,108 | 34,374 |
| 2011 | 8,473 | 34,675 | 43,148 |
| 2012 | 11,838 | 41,455 | 53,293 |
| 2013 | 15,888 | 44,188 | 60,076 |
| 2014 | 22,526 | 56,959 | 79,485 |
| Total | 64,991 | 205,385 | 270,376 |

Source: GAO analysis of U.S. Citizenship and Immigration Services data.| GAO-16-50

The number of principal affirmative applications and their eligible dependents has increased each year from fiscal years 2010 through 2014. The number of principal affirmative applications filed has increased from 28,108 in fiscal year 2010 to 56,959 in fiscal year 2014, a 103 percent increase. The portion of affirmative asylum applicants noted as dependents increased from 6,266 in fiscal year 2010 to 22,526 in fiscal year 2014, a 259 percent increase. Table 2 shows the number of principal and dependent affirmative asylum applications filed each year for fiscal years 2010 through 2014.

Asylum applications (including principal applicants and their eligible dependents) filed with EOIR—affirmative applications referred from USCIS and defensive applications—increased from 32,830 in fiscal year 2010 to 41,920 in fiscal year 2014, an increase of 28 percent. Table 3 shows the number of affirmative and defensive asylum cases EOIR received from fiscal years 2010 through 2014. The number of affirmative applications USCIS referred to EOIR increased from 20,086 in fiscal year 2010 to 25,907 in fiscal year 2012, and decreased from fiscal year 2012 to fiscal year 2014. Asylum Division officials attribute the decrease in affirmative asylum cases referred to EOIR to the increased number of credible fear and reasonable fear cases USCIS has received, which has caused USCIS to divert resources away from affirmative asylum cases and adjudicate fewer affirmative asylum cases overall. The number of credible fear and reasonable fear cases increased from 11,019 in fiscal year 2010 to 60,085 in fiscal year 2014, an increase of 445 percent.[52]

**Table 3. Asylum Applications Filed with the Executive Office for Immigration Review (EOIR), Fiscal Years 2010 through 2014**

| Fiscal year | Affirmative applications referred to EOIR from U.S. Citizens hip and Immigration Services | Defensive applications filed with EOIR | Total |
|---|---|---|---|
| 2010 | 20,086 | 12,744 | **32,830** |
| 2011 | 24,949 | 17,861 | **42,810** |
| 2012 | 25,907 | 19,648 | **45,555** |
| 2013 | 17,394 | 22,535 | **39,929** |
| 2014 | 13,253 | 28,667 | **41,920** |
| **Total** | **101,589** | **101,455** | **203,044** |

Source: GAO analysis of EOIR data.|GAO-16-50.

Source: GAO analysis of U.S. Citizenship and Immigration Services data; Map Resources (map). | GAO-16-50

Figure 4. Top 10 Countries of Nationality of Affirmative Asylum Applicants, Fiscal Years 2010 through 2014.

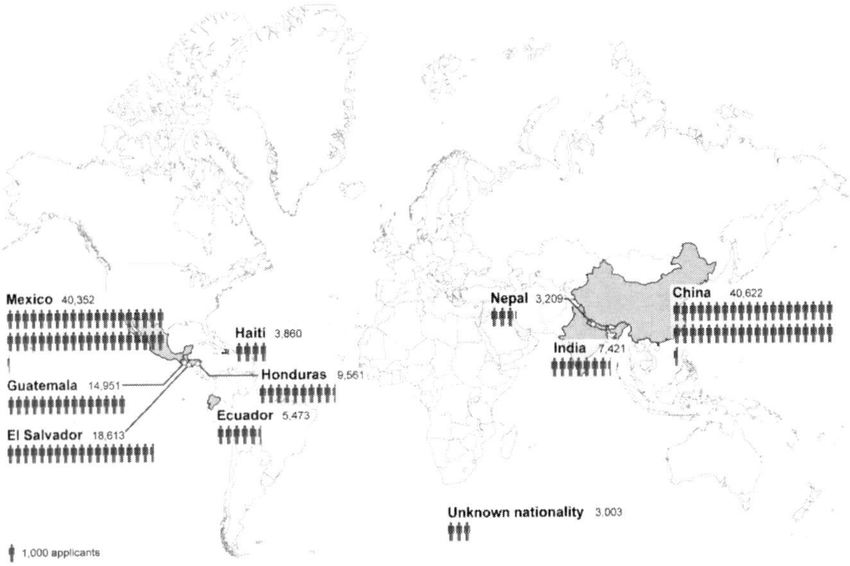


Source: GAO analysis of Executive Office for Immigration Review data; Map Resources (map).|GAO-16-50.

Figure 5. Top 10 Countries of Nationality of Asylum Applications File d with the Executive Office for Immigration Review, Fiscal Years 2010 through 2014.

## Asylum Applicant Characteristics Vary By Country of Nationality and Location

### *Country of Nationality*

From fiscal year 2010 through fiscal year 2014, China accounted for the largest number of affirmative asylum applicants (26 percent), followed by Mexico (13 percent) and Egypt (6 percent). Figure 4 shows the top 10 countries for affirmative asylum applications filed with USCIS.

From fiscal year 2010 through fiscal year 2014, China accounted for the largest number of asylum applicants filing with EOIR (20 percent), followed by Mexico (20 percent) and El Salvador (9 percent). Figure 5 shows the top 10 countries for asylum applicants filing with EOIR.

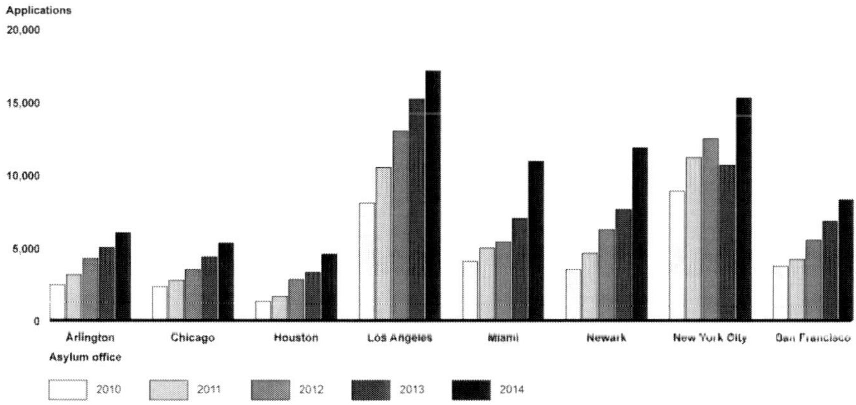


Source: GAO analysis of U.S. Citizenship and Immigration Services data. | GAO-16-50

Figure 6. Affirmative Asylum Applications Received by Asylum Office, Fiscal Years 2010 through 2014.

### *Location Filed*

USCIS has eight asylum offices across the United States and, as of April 2015, 353 asylum officers who are responsible for adjudicating affirmative asylum claims. The number of affirmative asylum applications filed per USCIS office varied widely. From fiscal years 2010 through 2014, the New York and Los Angeles asylum offices accounted for 45 percent of all affirmative asylum applications filed. The number of affirmative asylum applications filed in Newark and Los Angeles has grown more than in any other asylum office during this time, with a total increase of 8,352 and 9,070 applications. Figure 6 shows affirmative asylum applications received by each USCIS asylum office from fiscal year 2010 through fiscal year 2014.

## USCIS Has a Backlog of More than 100,000 Principal Affirmative Asylum Applications, Most of Which Have Exceeded Required Time Frames for Adjudication

Final administrative adjudication of an asylum application, not including administrative appeals, is to be completed within 180 days after filing, absent exceptional circumstances and not including any delays requested or caused by the applicant, or, where applicable, the amount of time between issuance of a request for evidence and the receipt of the applicant's response.[53] USCIS's backlog of principal affirmative asylum applications as of September 2015 was 106,121. Of those pending cases, 64,254 (61 percent) have exceeded the 180-day requirement. In addition, the number of affirmative asylum cases that were adjudicated in more than 180 days has increased from fiscal years 2010 through 2014. Figure 7 shows the number of affirmative asylum applications adjudicated from fiscal years 2010 through 2014 where USCIS's adjudication exceeded 180 days.

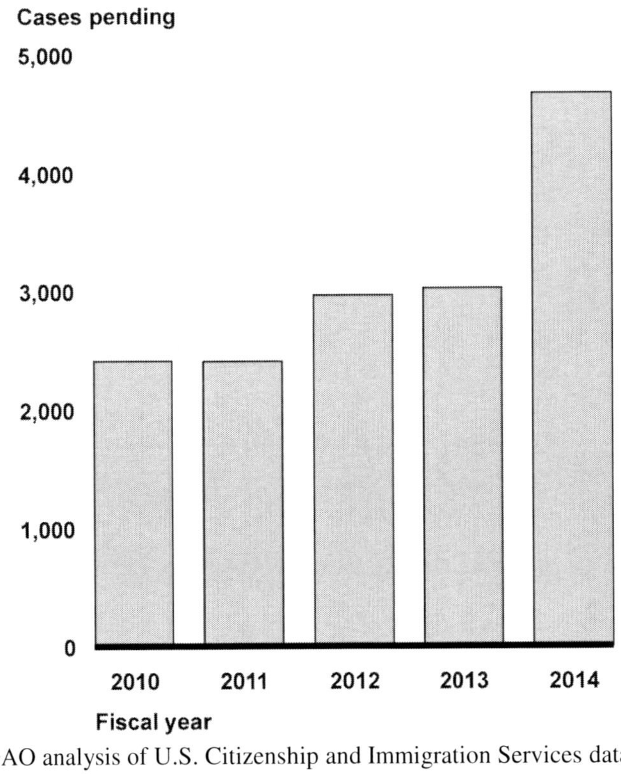


Source: GAO analysis of U.S. Citizenship and Immigration Services data.|GAO-16-50.
Note: This figure includes only those applications that USCIS adjudicated and does not include applications still pending adjudication as of September 2015.

Figure 7. Affirmative Asylum Applications Adjudicate d in More than 180 Days, Fiscal Years 2010 through 2014.

According to Asylum Division officials, several factors have affected USCIS's ability to adjudicate affirmative asylum applications in a timely manner. For example, officials stated that they have diverted resources to address the growth in credible fear and reasonable fear cases, which increased by over 400 percent from fiscal year 2010 through fiscal year 2014. In addition, these officials stated that they had prioritized applications from unaccompanied alien children based on the time sensitivity of such cases.[54] Asylum Division officials said that this diversion of resources and prioritization of these claims contributed to the increasing backlog of affirmative asylum applications. Asylum Division officials stated that the increasing number of affirmative applications in recent years has also had significant implications for the workload of USCIS's asylum offices, and that USCIS plans to hire additional staff to help address the current level of applications and the increasing backlog.

# DHS AND DOJ HAVE LIMITED CAPABILITIES TO DETECT AND PREVENT ASYLUM FRAUD

## DHS and DOJ Have Established Dedicated Antifraud Entities

Both DHS and DOJ have established dedicated antifraud entities, a leading practice for managing fraud risks. Our Fraud Framework states that a leading practice for managing fraud risks is to establish a dedicated entity to design and oversee fraud risk management activities.[55] Within DHS, USCIS created FDNS in 2004 to help ensure immigration benefits are not granted to individuals who pose a threat to national security or public safety or who seek to defraud the immigration system. As of fiscal year 2015, USCIS has deployed 35 FDNS immigration officers and 4 supervisory immigration officers working across all eight asylum offices. FDNS immigration officers working in asylum offices are tasked with conducting background checks to resolve national security "hits" and fraud concerns, which arise when asylum officers conduct required background checks of asylum applicants; addressing fraud-related leads provided by asylum officers and other sources; and liaising with law enforcement entities, such as HSI, to provide logistical support in law enforcement and national security matters.[56]

In September 2007, DOJ established an EOIR antifraud officer through regulation.[57] The regulation states that the antifraud officer is to (1) serve as a point of contact relating to concerns about fraud, particularly with respect to fraudulent applications or documents affecting multiple removal proceedings, applications for relief from removal, appeals, or other proceedings before EOIR; (2) coordinate with DHS and DOJ investigative authorities with respect to the identification of and response to fraud; and (3) notify EOIR's Disciplinary Counsel and other appropriate authorities as to instances of fraud, misrepresentation, or abuse related to an attorney or accredited representative.[58] The activities of the antifraud officer (also known as the Fraud Prevention Counsel) and supporting staff collectively are referred to as the Fraud and Abuse Prevention Program. According to EOIR's Fraud Prevention Program fact sheet, the goal of the program is to protect the integrity of EOIR and other immigration proceedings by promoting efforts to deter fraud and provide a systematic response to identifying and referring instances of suspected fraud and abuse. In practice, according to the Fraud Prevention Counsel, they collect data and review records of proceedings in response to reports of suspected fraud. In addition, through the program, EOIR coordinates with law enforcement agencies to refer appropriate matters for investigation and assist in fraud investigations and prosecutions. Further, the program provides training for EOIR staff, including immigration judges, and distributes a monthly newsletter about fraud related activity. Table 4 shows the total number of complaints received, the number of case files opened, and the number of asylum-related case files opened from fiscal year 2010 through fiscal year 2014. EOIR's Fraud and Abuse Prevention Program tracks the number of complaints it receives about potential fraud, but does not create a formal case file if the complaint or request for assistance can be closed quickly with minimal investment of staff time. As a result, not every complaint has a corresponding file.[59]

**Table 4. Executive Office for Immigration Review (EOIR) Fraud and Abuse Prevention Program Com plaints Received and Case Files Opened, Fiscal Years 2010 through 2014**

| Fiscal year | Com plaints received | Case files opened | Asylum –related case files opened |
|---|---|---|---|
| 2010 | 92 | 53 | 9 |
| 2011 | 98 | 38 | 4 |
| 2012 | 88 | 21 | 7 |
| 2013 | 66 | 16 | 3 |
| 2014 | 71 | 25 | 7 |

Source: GAO analysis of EOIR data and EOIR Fraud Prevention Program case files. | GAO 16-50.

Note: EOIR's Fraud Prevention Counsel creates a case file if the Fraud and Abuse Prevention Program performs substantive work pursuant to a complaint. As a result, not every complaint has a corresponding case file.

This table includes complaints received, and requests for assistance made to the Fraud and Abuse Prevention Program. Prior to March 2010, EOIR did not track all complaints received, or requests for assistance; therefore, the number of complaints in fiscal year 2010 may be greater.

## USCIS Has Not Assessed Fraud Risks across Affirmative Asylum Claims

USCIS has not assessed fraud risks across the affirmative asylum application process. The Fraud Framework states that it is a leading practice for agencies to create an organizational culture to combat fraud at all levels and designate an entity to lead fraud risk management activities, such as planning regular fraud risk assessments to determine a fraud risk profile for their program.[60] There is no universally accepted approach for conducting fraud risk assessments, since circumstances among programs vary; however, assessing fraud risks generally involves five actions: identifying inherent fraud risks affecting the program, assessing the likelihood and impact of those fraud risks, determining fraud risk tolerance, examining the suitability of existing fraud controls and prioritizing residual fraud risks, and documenting the program's fraud risk profile. Depending on the nature of the program, the frequency with which antifraud entities update the assessment can range from 1 to 5 years.[61]

USCIS officials stated that USCIS has not conducted an enterprise-wide fraud risk assessment, as the agency has implemented individual activities that demonstrate that it is conducting risk assessments. According to USCIS officials, such activities include the prescreening of asylum applications by FDNS immigration officers in advance of asylum interviews, security and background checks of applicants, information sharing agreements between the United States and other countries to access records related to persons of interest, fraud training for asylum officers, and mechanisms for the referral of cases to FDNS and to other investigative entities. Investigations of fraud are usually conducted after fraud has occurred and asylum may or may not have been granted. While these efforts can help USCIS detect and investigate potential fraud in individual asylum applications, they do not position USCIS to assess fraud risks across the affirmative asylum application process. The mentioned mechanisms are all tools with which to support a fraud risk assessment; however, an enterprise-wide fraud risk assessment would provide further information on the inherent risks across all applications. For example, asylum officers face fraud risks because they must make decisions, at times, with little or no documentation to support or refute an applicant's claim. As noted in the Fraud Framework, fraud risk management activities such as a fraud risk assessment may be incorporated into or aligned with internal activities and strategic objectives already in place, and information on fraud trends and lessons learned can be used to improve the design and implementation of fraud risk management activities.[62] Further, regular fraud risk assessments will help identify fraud vulnerabilities before any actual fraud occurs, and allow management to take steps to strengthen controls for fraud. Various cases of asylum fraud demonstrate ways in which applicants and preparers have sought to exploit the asylum system and help illustrate fraud risks in the affirmative asylum application process, especially risks associated with attorney and preparer fraud. For example,

- As of March 2014, a joint fraud investigation led by the U.S. Attorney's Office for the Southern District of New York, the Federal Bureau of Investigation (FBI), the New York City Police Department, and USCIS, known as Operation Fiction Writer, resulted in charges against 30 defendants, including 8 attorneys, for their alleged participation in immigration fraud schemes in New York City. According to discussions with USCIS officials and a FBI press release, allegations regarding these defendants generally involved the preparation of fraudulent asylum applications that often followed one of three fact patterns: (1) forced abortions performed pursuant to China's family planning policy; (2) persecution based on the applicant's belief in Christianity; or (3) political or ideological persecution, typically for membership in China's Democratic Party or followers of Falun Gong. Attorneys and preparers charged in Operation Fiction Writer filed 5,773 affirmative asylum applications with USCIS, and USCIS granted asylum to 829 of those affirmative asylum applicants.[63] According to EOIR data, 3,709 individuals who were connected to attorneys and preparers convicted in Operation Fiction Writer were granted asylum in immigration court; this includes both affirmative asylum claims referred from USCIS as well as defensive asylum claims.

- An asylum fraud investigation prompted in 2009 and led by the Los Angeles asylum office resulted in the indictment and subsequent conviction of two immigration consultants. The indictment alleged that the two consultants charged approximately $6,500 to prepare and file applications on behalf of Chinese nationals seeking asylum in the United States. These applications falsely claimed that the applicants had fled China because of persecution for their Christian beliefs. HSI investigators have linked the consultants to more than 800 asylum applications filed since 2000.

In 2002, we reported that the legacy Immigration and Naturalization Service (INS) did not know the extent of immigration benefit fraud.[64] In response, INS initiated the Benefit Fraud Assessment program in 2002 to measure the integrity of specific nonimmigrant and immigrant applications by conducting administrative inquiries on randomly selected cases, but later discontinued the effort because of competing priorities after the terrorist attacks of September 11, 2001. USCIS reinitiated the Benefit Fraud Assessment program through FDNS in 2005 and, in November 2009, FDNS drafted a Benefit Fraud and Compliance Assessment (BFCA) on asylum for internal USCIS discussion. The assessment was intended to study the scope and types of fraud associated with the Form I-589, determine the relative utility of a number of fraud detection methods, and assess the extent to which asylum officers were using the fraud detection measures that were part of the adjudication process at the time. However, FDNS did not release the report to external parties because of questions about the validity and soundness of the methodology used in the BFCA. In 2010, USCIS's Office of Policy and Strategy assumed responsibility for future BFCAs. USCIS contracted for a review of the BFCA on asylum, and in September 2012, the contractor reported that USCIS should not release the BFCA and made recommendations to improve future studies. For example, the contractor reported that the assessment process was not well planned and had methodological problems and issues with clarity. [65]

As of September 2015, officials from the Office of Policy and Strategy stated that USCIS is renaming the BFCA as the Immigration Benefit Fraud Assessment (IBFA). USCIS officials stated that under the new IBFA program, they plan to design rigorous research methods to provide fraud rates for selected benefit types. Office of Policy and Strategy officials did not provide a timeframe regarding the completion of future IBFA studies, and stated that USCIS has no plans to conduct an IBFA on asylum because they are still working to develop a framework for selecting which immigration benefits to study in the future. Office of Policy and Strategy officials said that the IBFA is not a fraud risk assessment and that their efforts will not be used to assess the risk of fraud in benefit types but will, instead, estimate the fraud rate of a given benefit. USCIS officials stated that they do not view the IBFA as a fraud risk assessment and that asylum is more difficult to study than other immigration benefits because asylum claims are generally based on testimonial evidence, making it more difficult to prove fraud than with other claims, and involve confidentiality restrictions.[66]

*Standards for Internal Control in the Federal Government* states that entities should comprehensively identify risks at both the entity-wide and activity levels. A risk assessment will help to determine how risks should be managed through the identification and analysis of relevant risks associated with achieving agency objectives.[67] Because USCIS must balance its mission to protect those with genuine asylum claims with the need to prevent ineligible individuals from fraudulently obtaining asylum, USCIS could benefit from assessing fraud risks across its asylum adjudication process, particularly to assess the fraud risk tolerance of the asylum system—a leading practice for assessing fraud risks. The Fraud Framework states that managers who effectively assess fraud risks attempt to fully consider the specific fraud risks the agency or program faces, analyze the potential likelihood and impact of fraud schemes, and document prioritized fraud risks. The aforementioned examples of fraud investigations further illustrate the need for preventive measures of fraud detection within the asylum program. In addition, risk tolerance reflects management's willingness to accept a higher level of fraud risk based on the circumstances and objectives of the program. For example, to protect genuine asylum applicants who may be unable to provide documents supporting their applications, asylum law states that testimonial information alone can be sufficient for asylum applicants to meet the burden of proof for establishing asylum eligibility.[68]

According to USCIS training materials for new asylum officers, asylum officers are to interview applicants in a nonadversarial manner and assume a cooperative approach as the applicant seeks to establish his or her eligibility.[69] USCIS instructs asylum officers, when assessing whether an applicant has provided sufficient detail about his or her claim, to account for the amount of time that has elapsed since the events occurred; the possible effects of trauma; the applicant's background, education, and culture; and any other factors that might impair the applicant's memory. The Asylum Division Branch Chief said that while this cooperative approach aims to protect genuine asylees, it can also create favorable circumstances for ineligible individuals who seek to file fraudulent claims, and asylum officers in seven of the eight asylum offices we spoke with told us that they have granted asylum in cases in which they suspected fraud.[70] For example, three asylum offices said that it was difficult to prove fraud existed in the asylum application. Although there are individual efforts in place to detect fraud, an enterprise-wide assessment of fraud risk could better inform asylum officers when adjudicating cases, and influence training materials regarding such subjects as country conditions. Without regularly assessing fraud risks and determining the fraud risk tolerance of the USCIS asylum adjudication process, USCIS does not have complete information on the inherent fraud risks that may affect the integrity of the affirmative asylum application process and therefore does not have reasonable assurance that it has implemented controls to mitigate those risks. Moreover, given the growth in affirmative asylum applications in recent years, and the USCIS pending caseload of over 100,000 affirmative asylum cases to adjudicate, assessing program-wide fraud risks could help USCIS target its fraud prevention efforts to those areas that are of highest risk in accordance with its fraud risk tolerance.

## EOIR Has Not Assessed Fraud Risks across Asylum Applications in the Immigration Courts

EOIR has not assessed the fraud risks associated with asylum applications across immigration courts. EOIR's immigration judges serve as the sole adjudicators for all defensive asylum claims made in the immigration courts and affirmative asylum applications referred by USCIS's asylum officers.[71] Asylum fraud-related cases mentioned below have demonstrated that EOIR faces fraud risks in these claims. The Fraud Framework states that it is a leading practice for agencies to create an organizational culture to combat fraud at all levels and designate an entity to lead fraud risk management activities, such as planning regular fraud risk assessments to determine a fraud risk profile for their program.[72] EOIR officials told us that the Fraud and Abuse Prevention Program has not assessed fraud risks across asylum applications in the immigration courts because it lacks financial and human resources. EOIR's Fraud and Abuse Prevention Program is composed of one full- time fraud prevention counsel, who serves as the antifraud officer pursuant to EOIR's regulations, one part-time attorney, and several student interns. Therefore, according to EOIR's antifraud officer, the Fraud and Abuse

Prevention Program has primarily served as an in-house referral system for EOIR employees. EOIR officials also stated that it would be difficult to conduct a fraud risk assessment across immigration courts because fraud is difficult to measure.

EOIR has efforts in place to assess fraud identified and referred to the Fraud and Abuse Prevention Program, such as reviewing fraud referrals once received, reviewing records of proceedings, and making referrals to law enforcement entities for investigation. However, recent asylum fraud cases identified in the program's case files illustrate the presence of fraud risks across asylum applications in immigration courts. For example, according to EOIR data, immigration judges granted asylum to 3,709 individuals who were connected to attorneys and preparers convicted in Operation Fiction Writer.[73] In addition, almost 20 percent (30 of 153) of EOIR's Fraud and Abuse Prevention Case files opened in fiscal year 2010 through fiscal year 2014 were related to asylum fraud. Further, 17 of the 30 case files we reviewed contained multiple types of immigration fraud, including document fraud and benefit fraud, as well as potential fraud in connection with the unauthorized practice of law.[74] As discussed above and in appendix II, the Fraud Framework states that it is a leading practice for agencies to plan regular fraud risk assessments and determine a fraud risk profile for their programs.[75] Managers who effectively assess fraud risks attempt to fully consider the specific fraud risks the agency or program faces, analyze the potential likelihood and impact of fraud schemes, and document prioritized fraud risks. The Fraud Framework states that it is a leading practice for an agency to designate an antifraud entity as a repository of knowledge for fraud risk, and to tailor its fraud risk assessments process to the program in question. Factors such as size, resources, maturity of the program, and experience in managing fraud risks can influence how an agency plans its fraud risk assessment. Although quantitative techniques are generally more precise than qualitative methods, when resource constraints, expertise, or other circumstances prohibit the use of statistical analysis for assessing fraud risks, other quantitative or qualitative techniques can still be informative. For example, the Fraud Framework discusses the use of risk scoring to quantify the likelihood and effect of particular fraud risks. Our analysis of the Fraud and Abuse Prevention case files indicate that there are multiple types of fraud that could be assessed through a fraud risk assessment such as benefit fraud, marriage fraud, and fraud in connection with the unauthorized practice of law.

We recognize that it can be difficult to measure or assess fraud risks and that EOIR has limited resources for assessing and addressing such risks. However, as noted in the framework, fraud risk management activities such as a fraud risk assessment may be incorporated into or aligned with internal activities and strategic objectives already in place, and information on fraud trends and lessons learned can be used to improve the design and implementation of fraud risk management activities.[76] Proactive fraud risk management would also mitigate the risk for fraud so that it is less likely to occur. Without regularly identifying and assessing fraud risks and determining the fraud risk tolerance in immigration courts, EOIR does not have complete information on the inherent fraud risks that may affect the integrity of the defensive asylum process and therefore does not have reasonable assurance that it has implemented controls to mitigate those risks.

In addition, as noted in our framework, fraud risk assessments can provide partners and stakeholders with information that can also assist in their operations and efforts. Managers who effectively manage fraud risks collaborate and communicate with internal and external stakeholders to share information on fraud risks, emerging fraud schemes, and lessons learned related to fraud control activities.[77] ICE OPLA attorneys are responsible for presenting evidence of and proving fraud in immigration court, and ICE HSI investigates cases of asylum fraud that are referred from the immigration courts. EOIR officials said that its Office of Planning Analysis and Statistics has previously provided data for OPLA attorneys to assist in court proceedings and investigations when requested. ICE OPLA attorneys we interviewed at all four of the field offices we visited told us that if asylum fraud is detected, it is difficult to prove in immigration court. Attorneys at two of the offices we visited stated that, in their experience, proving fraud requires an immense amount of time and evidence. ICE OPLA attorneys in one location stated that, as a result of factors such as these, there is no incentive for them to litigate asylum fraud cases. An EOIR fraud risk assessment could help ICE OPLA, for example, better educate OPLA attorneys about fraud risks as they represent the government in immigration court proceedings. Moreover, managers can use the fraud risk assessment process to determine the extent to which controls may no longer be relevant or cost-effective. Thus, a fraud risk assessment would help EOIR ensure that it is targeting its limited fraud prevention resources effectively.

## USCIS Does Not Have Complete or Readily Available Data on FDNS's Efforts to Combat Asylum Fraud

Within USCIS, FDNS does not have complete or readily available data on fraud referrals and requests for assistance from asylum officers and on its asylum fraud-related investigations and the outcomes of those investigations. First, with regard to data on fraud referrals and requests for assistance from asylum officers, such data are not consistently entered into the FDNS Data System (FDNS-DS), which is USCIS's agency-wide database for maintaining data and information on all FDNS activities, including activities associated with asylum fraud investigations. According to training materials for new asylum officers, if an asylum officer has questions about a potential fraud indicator while adjudicating an affirmative asylum claim, he or she can submit a request for assistance to the FDNS immigration officers in his or her asylum office. For example, FDNS may be able to provide additional information about an asylum applicant by conducting searches of databases that asylum officers cannot access. In addition, FDNS immigration officers can conduct document reviews and analyses of the application to determine whether fraud may exist. According to USCIS training materials for new asylum officers, each asylum office may have a different process for requesting assistance from FDNS. According to the training materials, as well as FDNS immigration officers we spoke with in asylum offices, officers typically deliver their responses to a request for assistance informally, such as by orally communicating the results of their reviews to asylum officers without supporting documentation. FDNS's fraud detection standard operating procedures state that requests for assistance are to be entered into FDNS-DS.[78] However, according to FDNS officials in headquarters and field offices, these requests are not consistently entered into FDNS-DS. Additionally, while the requests may be tracked at the office level within individual asylum offices, they are not otherwise tracked across individual offices by either the Asylum Division or FDNS.

Moreover, according to the training materials for new asylum officers, in cases where a fraud indicator cannot be quickly resolved by FDNS, such as a suspicion of fraud or a complicated case needing more research by FDNS, the asylum officer is to complete a Fraud Referral Sheet. After receiving a referral, FDNS is to determine whether the referral has sufficient information to warrant further investigation. According to FDNS's fraud detection standard operating procedures, FDNS immigration officers are to enter all fraud referrals, including those that they will decline, into FDNS-DS to accurately record the number of referrals received, track their processing, and support quality assurance. However, in practice, FDNS headquarters officials stated that officers typically enter referrals into FDNS-DS as "leads" only if they warrant additional investigation. While some FDNS immigration officers track referrals at the asylum office level, not all referrals are entered into the agency-wide FDNS-DS. As a result, FDNS-DS does not have complete data on the number of fraud referrals or requests for assistance in each asylum office or across asylum offices, making it difficult to determine the extent to which asylum officers request assistance from FDNS on fraud- related questions or suspicions in adjudicating asylum applications.

Second, FDNS does not have readily available data on the number of asylum fraud cases it investigates, the number of asylum fraud cases in which FDNS immigration officers find asylum fraud, or the number of asylum fraud cases that FDNS refers to HSI for further investigation. According to FDNS's fraud detection standard operating procedures, if FDNS immigration officers determine that a referral warrants additional investigation, they are to enter that referral into FDNS-DS as a fraud lead. If, after conducting research and analyzing the information associated with a lead, the immigration officer determines that a reasonable suspicion of fraud is articulated and actionable, the lead is elevated to a case. FDNS immigration officers may also enter a referral into the database directly as a case if a reasonable suspicion of fraud is articulated and actionable. According to FDNS officials, FDNS data entry rules require that all immigration forms associated with an individual under investigation be included with the individual's FDNS-DS case. Not every immigration form associated with an individual or case is the basis for fraud in that case and a case may include multiple immigration forms. For example, if FDNS opened a case about an individual who was legitimately granted asylum, but who later committed marriage fraud, the FDNS-DS case record would include both the legitimate asylum application and the fraudulent marriage-based benefit application.[79] Furthermore, according to FDNS officials, when an immigration officer first enters a case into FDNS-DS, he or she is to categorize the type of fraud that is the subject of the case. For example, the officer would categorize an asylum fraud case as "benefit fraud—asylum" in FDNS-DS. However, FDNS officials stated that, because of the limitations of FDNS- DS, each case record can only reflect one type of fraud at a time, although the system does have the capacity to record and report updates if, for example, the type of fraud associated with a record is changed. FDNS officials stated that a case that begins as an asylum fraud investigation might ultimately result in a fraud finding or referral to HSI based on another type of fraud, such as marriage fraud. FDNS officials stated that if asylum fraud is not the most egregious type of benefit fraud in a particular investigation, the investigation may not be categorized as asylum fraud in FDNS-DS.

Because of the limitations of FDNS-DS, FDNS headquarters officials stated that the number of FDNS-DS records categorized as "benefit fraud—asylum" may not accurately represent the number of asylum fraud investigations completed by FDNS or the number of asylum fraud cases FDNS referred to HSI. FDNS headquarters officials stated that making such a determination would require a manual review of each case record in FDNS-DS categorized as "benefit fraud—asylum" or associated with an I-589, the asylum application. Both of these data fields indicate that the case record could be, but is not necessarily, related to an investigation of asylum fraud. Without this manual review, a process that would be extremely labor-intensive, FDNS cannot determine which immigration forms or benefit types are the subject of an investigation or of a referral from FDNS to HSI. According to FDNS data from FDNS-DS, in fiscal year 2014, FDNS opened 336 cases in which the individual implicated was associated with an asylum application, either as the applicant or as an attorney, preparer, or interpreter assisting the applicant, and FDNS found fraud in 210 of those cases. However, FDNS cannot readily determine how many of those cases involved asylum fraud without manually reviewing each individual case.

*Standards for Internal Control in the Federal Government* states that agencies must have relevant, reliable, and timely information to determine whether their operations are performing as expected.[80] Without complete data on the number of requests for assistance from asylum officers to FDNS, the number of referrals that asylum officers submit to FDNS, and the number of FDNS investigations that result in a finding of asylum fraud, USCIS officials cannot determine how often the fraud referral process is used or how often it results in a finding of asylum fraud. Complete data on these matters would also help support a fraud risk assessment, as previously discussed, by giving USCIS additional information about fraud schemes and trends from fraud detection activities so that officials can ensure that fraud detection activities are appropriately tailored to the agency's risk profile.

## USCIS Has Limited Capability to Detect Fraud in Affirmative Asylum Applications

### *USCIS's Capability to Identify Patterns of Fraud across Asylum Applications is Limited*

USCIS uses various tools to attempt to identify fraud in specific affirmative asylum applications. USCIS uses some of these tools, such as biometric identity verification and biographic and biometric background and security checks, on all asylum applications. These tools help asylum officers identify fraud by confirming the applicant's identity and identifying prior criminal convictions, among other things. Further, the Asylum Division and FDNS have some additional tools available that officers can use to address cases with indicators of fraud; however, our analysis of HSI and USCIS data indicates that some of these tools are of limited utility and use. Specifically, USCIS guidance for FDNS immigration officers discusses the use of two fraud detection tools for verifying applicants' claims and supporting documents—the ICE HSI Forensic Laboratory and overseas verification. HSI's Forensic Laboratory specializes in determining the authenticity of documents and identifying the presence of alterations within those documents. In particular, the Forensic Laboratory specializes in verifying travel and identity documents, such as passports, visas, driver's licenses, and identification cards. However, according to Forensic Laboratory guidance for document submission issued in 2010, the Forensic Laboratory prioritizes matters of national security, criminal violations, cases involving people who have been detained, and cases involving multiple incidents related to organized fraudulent activity. According to Forensic Laboratory officials, the Forensic Laboratory may accept non-priority requests on a case-by-case basis. Asylum applications, which are not criminal cases and usually involve nondetained applicants, therefore generally do not fit within the laboratory's priorities, according to USCIS and ICE officials. Furthermore, both FDNS and Forensic Laboratory officials stated that the Forensic Laboratory generally cannot verify some types of documents commonly submitted as support for asylum claims, such as foreign police reports and medical records. Forensic Laboratory officials told us that these documents are difficult to authenticate because the laboratory does not have genuine exemplar documents for comparison purposes and because the documents are typically not standardized and do not have security features that can be verified by forensic examination. According to HSI and Asylum Division officials, neither the Forensic Laboratory nor the Asylum Division tracks submissions to the Forensic Laboratory specific to asylum applications; however, according to HSI data, USCIS submitted 60 cases to the Forensic Laboratory in fiscal year 2014 across all immigration benefits. Asylum officers we interviewed in all eight asylum offices said that they rarely use the Forensic Laboratory, in part because of untimely and inconclusive responses.

Asylum officers may also submit documents for overseas verification, either by USCIS officers overseas or, in areas where USCIS does not have an overseas presence, by State Department consular officers. Overseas verification refers to the verification of events, education, or work experience that occurred in a foreign country or the authentication of a document or information that originated overseas. From fiscal years 2010 through 2014, asylum offices submitted 111 requests to either USCIS officers or State Department consular officers for overseas verification. Asylum officers we interviewed in all eight asylum offices stated that they rarely use overseas verification, in part because they do not receive responses to their requests in a timely manner. In addition, asylum confidentiality restrictions limit the extent to which asylum officers can verify information overseas; USCIS and State Department personnel generally cannot share information contained in or pertaining to an asylum application outside the U.S. government in a manner that would disclose the fact that the individual applied for asylum in the United States. Furthermore, asylum officers told us that the outcome of asylum adjudications rarely hinges on the authenticity of a single document, so document verification may not change the outcome of a case.

Further, USCIS's tools for detecting patterns of fraud across affirmative asylum applications are limited because USCIS relies on a paper-based system for asylum applications. After the applicant submits a paper Form I-589 to USCIS, Service Center personnel input certain biographic information, such as the applicant's name, date of birth, and nationality, from the paper application into the RAPS database. Asylum office personnel use RAPS to track the application's status and facilitate interview scheduling. In some cases, FDNS immigration officers can use information from RAPS for fraud detection by creating reports of cases with certain biographic characteristics, thereby identifying cases for potential review. However, RAPS does not have the capability to detect fraud trends because, while it captures biographic data about an asylum applicant, it does not capture other key information that could be used to detect fraud. Such information could include the applicant's written statement, the reason for the applicant's claim, or the name of the applicant's interpreter. Asylum officers and FDNS immigration officers told us that they can identify potential fraud by manually analyzing trends across asylum applications they review. Because of USCIS's reliance on paper asylum applications, asylum officers and FDNS immigration officers use ad hoc, labor-intensive methods to detect such trends among asylum cases. For example, FDNS immigration officers at three of the eight asylum offices stated that they photocopy asylum applications and maintain hard-copy case files for analysis.[81] In our 2008 report on the asylum adjudication process, we surveyed asylum officers across all asylum offices and found that 61 percent of asylum officers stated that scanning all I-589s and using software to identify boilerplate language and trends was "greatly needed," and 16 percent said it was "moderately needed."[82]

According to the FDNS Branch Chief for USCIS's RAIO Directorate, automated analytic capabilities for asylum applications, such as tools to detect fraud indicators, would lead to significant increases in efficiencies for fraud detection and investigation. For example, since 2014, FDNS has been reviewing the asylum applications associated with Operation Fiction Writer. FDNS does not have automated analytic tools to review information. Rather, FDNS immigration officers must manually review hundreds of asylum applications, requiring large investments of time and resources. In our interviews with asylum officers, officers in all eight asylum offices stated that they would benefit from greater access to analytic tools. According to the FDNS Branch Chief for RAIO, an automated analytic capability for asylum applications is a "critical need" for fraud detection.[83]

As we previously reported, in 2005, USCIS embarked on its multiyear Transformation Program to transform its paper-based immigration benefits process to a system with electronic application filing, adjudication, and case management.[84] The main component of the program is the USCIS Electronic Immigration System (ELIS), which is to provide case management for adjudication of immigration benefits. However, USCIS has faced longstanding challenges in implementing its Transformation Program, which raise questions about the extent to which its eventual deployment will position USCIS to collect and maintain more readily-available data. In May 2015, we reported that USCIS expects the Transformation Program will cost up to $3.1 billion and be fully deployed no later than March 2019, which is an increase of approximately $1 billion, and a delay of more than 4 years from its initial July 2011 baseline.[85] USCIS's most recent Life Cycle Cost Estimate for the Transformation Program states that USCIS will not complete deploying functional capabilities for USCIS's humanitarian mission, which includes asylum, until September 2018. Officials from USCIS's Transformation Program told us that, as of June 2015, they have not yet developed business requirements for asylum adjudication in USCIS ELIS or determined how USCIS ELIS implementation will affect asylum adjudications because they are currently focused on developing and deploying USCIS ELIS for other immigration benefits.

Because USCIS has not yet developed business requirements for asylum in USCIS ELIS, it is too early to assess how the information contained in USCIS ELIS could facilitate USCIS's asylum fraud detection efforts. Additionally, as we reported in May 2015, USCIS's ability to effectively monitor USCIS ELIS program performance and make informed decisions about its implementation has been limited because department-level governance and oversight bodies were not using reliable program information to inform their program evaluations.[86] The Fraud Framework states that it is a leading practice for agencies to use data analytics to identify and monitor trends that may indicate fraud and use information to improve fraud risk management activities, such as addressing control vulnerabilities and improving training. [87] Identifying and implementing additional fraud detection tools, such as automated analytic software, could enable FDNS and asylum officers to detect fraud more readily while using limited resources more efficiently. Without such tools, FDNS immigration officers are not well positioned to identify cases associated with particular asylum fraud rings or aid in the investigation and prosecution of the attorneys, preparers, and interpreters who perpetrate asylum fraud.

### *FDNS Prescreens Asylum Applications in Some, but Not All, Asylum Offices*

Some asylum offices have strengthened their capability to detect and prevent fraud by using FDNS immigration officers to prescreen affirmative asylum applications; however, the use of this practice varies across asylum offices. Prescreening applications, that is, reviewing the application for potential fraud indicators in advance of the asylum interview, allows FDNS to identify fraud trends and detect patterns that may not be evident in a small sample of asylum applications. Asylum officers we spoke with in all eight asylum offices stated that they face time constraints in adjudicating asylum applications. For example, asylum officers we spoke with in three asylum offices stated that they have limited time to review the details of the applications that they are adjudicating in advance of the applicant interview.

Additionally, each asylum officer adjudicates approximately eight affirmative asylum applications per week. Therefore, an individual officer might not see patterns of fraud in single applications that would be visible if he or she were reviewing the entire universe of applications in each asylum office. For example, asylum officers or supervisors we spoke with in six of eight asylum offices stated that FDNS prescreening was, or would be, helpful in identifying fraud indicators or fraud trends.[88]

USCIS training materials state that it is important to identify indicators of fraud before the applicant's interview so that asylum officers can ask appropriate questions during the interview. Before an interview, asylum officers can consult with their supervisors or FDNS about indicators of potential fraud in an application; however, they are not required to do so. As previously discussed, consistent with the REAL ID Act of 2005, credible testimony from the asylum applicant may be sufficient, without corroboration, for the applicant to receive asylum.[89] Asylum officers are to raise discrepancies, inconsistencies, or identified fraud in the asylum application during the interview, and upon completion of the interview, the applicant or the applicant's representative must have an opportunity to respond to the evidence presented.[90] When FDNS does not prescreen applications, the asylum officer is responsible for identifying potential fraud in the application prior to the interview and using that information during the interview to assess the applicant's credibility unless he or she temporarily pauses the interview to seek support from supervisors or FDNS. After an interview, the asylum officer may call applicants back to answer additional questions before a decision is rendered or conduct a full reinterview with applicants. However, in two asylum offices, supervisory asylum officers we spoke with stated that they prefer not to reinterview applicants because doing so adds to their adjudication backlog. Supervisory asylum officers we spoke with in three asylum offices stated that they conduct reinterviews when needed or in particular circumstances. [91] In three offices where FDNS prescreens asylum applications for indicators of fraud, FDNS immigration officers we spoke with stated that FDNS provides information to the asylum officer about the nature of the potential fraud in the application in advance of the applicant interview. This allows the asylum officer to ask relevant questions during the interview; gives the applicant the opportunity to provide an explanation for any discrepancies, inconsistencies, or identified fraud in the file; and ensures that the asylum officer is in the strongest position to assess the credibility of the applicant. According to FDNS immigration officers we spoke with in two asylum offices, prescreening also allows FDNS to identify applications that are affiliated with attorneys, preparers, or interpreters under FDNS investigation.

FDNS immigration officers we interviewed in five of the eight asylum offices stated that they prescreen some affirmative asylum applications; one asylum office prescreens all applications; and two asylum offices do not prescreen applications.[92] FDNS officials stated that staffing and resource constraints, coupled with the increase in affirmative asylum applications in recent years, have made it difficult for FDNS to prescreen all asylum applications. For example, in January 2015, immigration officers in one asylum office that does not prescreen asylum applications developed a plan to begin prescreening, but were unable to implement the plan because of a lack of administrative resources. In the five offices that prescreen some applications, officers may select applications for prescreening at random or based on certain characteristics such as the applicant's country of origin. Immigration officers set their own prescreening priorities in most of these offices. In both offices that do not prescreen affirmative asylum applications, FDNS officials stated that prescreening would be helpful and is an effective system for identifying fraud patterns but that resource constraints and national security priorities have limited their ability to prescreen asylum applications. However, the asylum office that prescreens all asylum applications is also the office that received the most affirmative asylum applications from fiscal years 2010 to 2014, and from fiscal years 2010 to 2013, this office was staffed with two full-time FDNS immigration officers, which is equal to or less than the staffing of all other FDNS immigration officers in asylum offices in that time period. This office was able to prescreen all asylum applications even though it had similar staffing resources and a higher volume of asylum applications than any other asylum office. Moreover, the head of the Asylum Division stated that FDNS prescreening is helpful to asylum officers and that he would like FDNS to prescreen all asylum applications prior to the interview. The FDNS Branch Chief for RAIO also stated that she supported more robust prescreening of affirmative asylum applications and noted that the process would need to be tailored to the specific needs and resource levels for each office.

According to the Fraud Framework, designing and implementing specific control activities to prevent and detect fraud is a leading practice for managers.[93] Additionally, the framework states that preventive control activities generally offer the most cost-effective investment of resources and that, while targeted controls, such as prescreening, may be more costly than agencywide controls, such as general fraud detection responsibilities, targeted controls may lower the cost of identifying each instance of fraud because they are more effective than controls that are not targeted. Although prescreening asylum cases may require additional time from FDNS immigration officers, it could ultimately help save time and resources by helping FDNS officers build large-scale asylum fraud investigations and detect new fraud patterns in a timely manner. Moreover, prescreening could help save resources by identifying indicators of fraud before the asylum interview. This would allow asylum officers to ask relevant questions during the interview and reduce the need for time-consuming reinterviews, in which the asylum office requests that an applicant return for a second interview to address issues not covered in the initial interview. Requiring that FDNS immigration officers prescreen all affirmative asylum applications for indicators of fraud, to the extent that it is cost-effective and feasible, would allow FDNS to better detect any such indicators at the point where that information is most useful for preventing asylum fraud.

## FDNS Has Not Established Clear Responsibilities for Fraud Detection in Asylum Offices

FDNS has not established clear responsibilities related to fraud detection for its immigration officers in asylum offices, and FDNS fraud detection activities vary widely by asylum office. In March 2011, FDNS issued standard operating procedures for fraud detection, which describe the procedures that FDNS immigration officers are to follow when investigating referrals related to immigration benefit fraud, as well as the process for referring immigration benefit fraud cases to HSI or other government or law enforcement agencies. These standard operating procedures are intended to guide fraud detection in all USCIS adjudications, including those at Service Centers and Field Offices, in addition to asylum offices. However, the standard operating procedures do not provide further details or guidance on the roles and responsibilities of FDNS immigration officers working in asylum offices. According to RAIO officials, FDNS immigration officers working in asylum offices face unique fraud detection challenges and the standard operating procedures state that immigration officers working in asylum offices must be sensitive to the unique legal requirements and issues involved with asylee processing, such as confidentiality requirements. FDNS immigration officers we spoke with in all eight asylum offices stated that they have limited guidance about their roles and responsibilities with respect to fraud detection, and officers at seven of the eight offices stated that the limited guidance creates challenges for them in addressing asylum fraud.[94]

Further, some of the processes outlined in the standard operating procedures differ from the processes we observed FDNS immigration officers following during our site visits to asylum offices. For example, the procedures state that FDNS will refer single-scheme cases—that is, individual cases of fraud—to HSI when they involve an attorney, interpreter, or preparer. FDNS immigration officers we spoke with at seven of eight asylum offices told us that they generally do not submit single-scheme cases to HSI.[95] HSI officials we spoke with confirmed that they rarely accept single-scheme asylum fraud cases for investigation because single-scheme cases are difficult to prosecute, and the penalties for individual instances of fraud are low. In addition, FDNS immigration officers at three asylum offices expressed confusion about whether they were permitted to conduct site visits for asylum fraud investigations, which the standard operating procedures list as one of the duties of an immigration officer.[96] Site visits allow FDNS immigration officers to verify information presented in an asylum application, such as an applicant's home address. According to FDNS officials, immigration officers may have been confused because they were not permitted to conduct site visits in the past because of limited resources and concerns about officer safety. However, in September 2015, FDNS headquarters officials stated that officers are permitted to conduct site visits, as appropriate for case- specific needs, and the additional FDNS officers hired in 2014 helped address prior resource constraints. Further, the standard operating procedures do not discuss prescreening asylum cases in advance of the asylum interview; however, as we previously stated, we found that immigration officers at six of the eight asylum offices were prescreening at least some asylum applications.

Additionally, FDNS's fraud detection activities varied widely across the eight asylum offices. For example, one asylum office we visited was responsible for submitting 87 of the 111 total overseas verification requests submitted by asylum offices from fiscal years 2010 through 2014. FDNS immigration officers at this office told us that they regularly prescreened asylum cases for potential fraud indicators, tracked potential fraud indicators in internal spreadsheets, submitted fraud referrals to HSI, and testified about asylum fraud in immigration court at the request of ICE OPLA trial attorneys. In another asylum office we visited, FDNS immigration officers we spoke with told us that they devote "very little time" to fraud detection and investigation because they focus on national security priorities. Immigration officers at this office did not submit any overseas verification requests from fiscal years 2010 through 2014, nor do they regularly prescreen applications. Asylum officers from one asylum office we spoke with said they report identified fraud trends to FDNS immigration officers in their office, but FDNS does not take action on the referrals or disseminate fraud trends or feedback regarding fraud referrals. In another asylum office, asylum officers said that fraud referrals and fraud trends are discussed informally between individual asylum and FDNS officers.

USCIS issued guidance in December 2014 detailing FDNS's priorities for immigration officers in the field for fiscal year 2015. The guidance states that FDNS will develop, implement, and monitor policies and programs that enhance USCIS's ability to detect and resolve fraud issues. *Standards for Internal Control in the Federal Government* states that a good internal control environment requires that the agency's organizational structure clearly define key areas of authority and responsibility and establish appropriate lines of reporting.[97] Furthermore, the Fraud Framework states that effective managers of fraud risks establish roles and responsibilities for fraud detection activities and describe the fraud risk management activities intended to prevent, detect, and respond to fraud as part of an overall antifraud strategy.[98] According to FDNS officials, FDNS did not think it was necessary to issue asylum- specific guidance for some fraud detection activities, such as site visits, because the number of immigration officers assigned to asylum was so small in the past that immigration officers had very little time for fraud detection activities. However, between fiscal years 2014 and 2015, the number of FDNS immigration officers working in asylum offices more than doubled, from 18 to 39. This increase in staffing levels will allow FDNS immigration officers to devote more time to detecting asylum fraud, according to FDNS headquarters officials. Developing asylum-specific guidance on the fraud detection roles and responsibilities of FDNS immigration officers working in asylum offices would better position those officers to understand their fraud detection roles and responsibilities, tools that are available to them in carrying out those roles and responsibilities, and features that are unique to the asylum system.

## USCIS Provides Limited Fraud Training for Asylum Officers and Does Not Have a Mechanism for Conducting Ongoing Training Needs Assessments

### *USCIS Provides Limited Fraud Training for Asylum Officers*

USCIS training for asylum officers includes basic training for new asylum officers and weekly training for all asylum officers; however, these trainings include limited information on fraud as compared to other topics. The training program for asylum officers is comprised of three main components. First, new asylum officers participate in 3 weeks of self- paced RAIO Directorate and Asylum Division distance training in their respective asylum offices. Distance training consists of webinars and video teleconference presentations, and asylum officers are expected to read the training materials and complete exercises and quizzes in preparation for residential training. Second, asylum officers participate in a 6-week residential basic training program, which includes 3 weeks of RAIO Directorate training and 3 weeks of Asylum Division training. Both courses include classroom instruction, practical exercises, and mock interviews on a variety of topics, such as national security, case law, children's claims, gender-related claims, human trafficking, and interviewing. At the end of the residential training courses, new asylum officers must pass final exams about the course with a score of at least 70 percent. Third, USCIS policy requires asylum offices to allocate 4 hours per week for formal or informal training for asylum officers and supervisory asylum officers. The training can range from classroom instruction by the asylum office's Training Officer to individual study time that asylum officers can use to study case law, research country conditions affecting prospective asylees, and read new USCIS procedures and guidance. The Asylum Division requires Training Officers to track the date and topic of each weekly training session and report that information to Asylum Division headquarters on a quarterly basis.

Regarding the distance training and residential training for new officers, USCIS's training materials include some information related to identifying and addressing potential fraud. Specifically, the RAIO distance training includes a webinar about fraud, and during the RAIO residential training sessions, asylum officers receive classroom instruction on various topics such as interviewing, evidence, and gender-related claims. Asylum officers also participate in mock interviews. In addition, the Asylum Division residential training includes in-class instruction on the topics mentioned above, as well as on fraud-related issues. Asylum officers participate in practical exercises and mock interviews related to various topics. Specifically, during the Asylum Division residential training session, new asylum officers receive four hours of fraud training delivered via PowerPoint slide presentations taught by various FDNS officials. During this session, asylum officers also complete practical exercises related to the fraud referral sheet. According to USCIS officials, although each instructor has his or her own set of slides and may present the information in different formats or use different asylum case examples, the content of these slides does not vary among FDNS instructors and the instructors teach a core set of principles in each class. We analyzed the RAIO distance training webinar regarding fraud, as well as two presentations that USCIS provided to us as examples of those used during the Asylum Division's training session. We found that the slides contained information on fraud indicators and the fraud referral process and, in particular, one PowerPoint presentation defined fraud, listed types of asylum fraud, highlighted the FDNS fraud referral sheet, and provided examples of prior fraud investigations.

While the distance and residential training sessions include materials related to asylum fraud, these materials do not include the same level of detail, depth, or breadth as the written training modules for other RAIO and Asylum Division training sessions. These materials serve as reference materials for asylum officers after they begin to adjudicate cases. In particular, RAIO's written training modules on other topics, such as the modules on human trafficking and gender-related claims, provide more robust discussions of each topic, contain links to relevant laws, and include suggested supplemental reading materials. For example, the human trafficking module and Asylum Division supplement contains lists of suggested interview questions, a sample memo that asylum officers can use to document human trafficking concerns, and a sample asylum decision. The gender-related claims module contains substantive definitions of eight types of gender-based harm, proposed interview considerations and sample questions, and an extensive legal analysis of such claims. The materials used for RAIO and Asylum Division training on fraud provide useful information on how fraud is defined and how to make referrals of suspected fraud to FDNS; however, these materials do not include extensive definitions of fraud, a sample memo, a sample decision, or sample interview questions. For example, our review of RAIO and Asylum Division training materials showed that these materials do not explain how asylum officers are to interview applicants when they suspect fraud or document fraud when writing asylum decisions. Moreover, supervisory asylum officers and asylum officers at six of the eight asylum offices we spoke with stated that they need additional fraud training.[99] In particular, asylum officers in three offices cited a need for training on interviewing applicants in cases where they suspect fraud, and officers we spoke with at two offices cited a need for training on how to document and substantiate fraud in asylum decisions.

Prior to 2012, USCIS had a written fraud training module. USCIS redeveloped its asylum officer training in 2012 and, since that time, neither the RAIO Directorate nor Asylum Division distance or residential basic training course have been guided by a written module on asylum fraud. Other USCIS materials refer asylum officers to the pre-2012 written fraud training module, which is no longer in place. For example, the *Affirmative Asylum Procedures Manual* refers asylum officers to the basic training materials for further guidance and instruction on various subjects, including how to address fraudulent evidence in an asylum application. Further, five of the RAIO training modules on other topics—such as the modules covering the affirmative asylum process and procedures, decision making, and evidence—refer asylum officers to the pre-2012 fraud module for more details on how to address and detect fraud in asylum applications. In September 2015, Asylum Division officials told us that they were working to finalize an updated fraud training module, but stated that the module required additional review before being finalized. Officials were unable to provide a time frame for finalizing the module. Officials previously attributed these delays to vacancies in the senior FDNS positions overseeing RAIO and the Asylum Division who would need to approve the updated module. As of March 2015, those positions have been filled. In technical comments that USCIS provided to us on a draft of this report, USCIS stated that it expected to finalize the written training module by March 2016 and provide this training to asylum officers by September 2016. While these plans are a positive step, it is too soon to tell the extent to which the finalized module will address the limitations we and asylum officers identified.

Regarding ongoing training for asylum officers, according to Asylum Division officials, USCIS complements its basic training program by providing weekly training sessions on a variety of topics, including fraud issues. However, our analysis of quarterly Training Officer reports for all eight asylum offices in fiscal year 2014 found that 8 of 408 training sessions were reported as being dedicated to fraud, and four of the eight asylum offices did not report providing dedicated specific fraud training in fiscal year 2014. According to Asylum Division officials, many of the weekly training sessions in fiscal year 2014 focused on credible and reasonable fear because of the increased number of those cases. According to our analysis of the training reports, the most common use of weekly training time was staff meetings or cancellations of formal training for the week, and the second most common use was information on country conditions.[100] According to Asylum Division officials, training on country conditions can provide asylum officers with information they can use to detect fraud in interviews; however, these trainings are not directly focused on identifying fraud. Weekly training topics also included security checks, immigration and asylum law, and USCIS policy changes. Three asylum offices we spoke with said that weekly training was not helpful for asylum adjudications. In one office, for example, officers stated that the weekly training was not helpful for identifying fraud, and was a burden at times because of their adjudication workload.

The Fraud Framework states that it is a leading practice for agencies to design and implement specific controls to prevent and detect fraud, which include fraud awareness initiatives such as training.[101] Increasing managers' and employees' awareness of potential fraud schemes through training and education can serve a preventive purpose by helping to create a culture of integrity and fraud deterrence. Providing asylum officers with additional training on asylum fraud, including finalizing the fraud training module and asylum division supplement for new asylum officers, would better position to USCIS to ensure that asylum officers have the training and skills needed to detect and address fraud indicators.

***USCIS Does Not Have a Mechanism for Regularly Assessing Asylum Officer Training Needs***

USCIS has taken steps to assess training needs among asylum officers; however, USCIS has not conducted an agencywide training needs assessment for asylum officers since 2010. In 2008, we recommended that the Chief of the Asylum Division develop a framework for soliciting information in a structured and consistent manner on asylum officers' and supervisors' respective training needs.[102] In response to our recommendation, USCIS delivered an online training needs assessment to asylum officers and supervisors in July 2010 and committed to creating a training agenda by soliciting and evaluating training needs and priorities annually thereafter. However, USCIS has not conducted regular training needs assessments since 2010. In 2012, as part of an effort to redesign its training programs, RAIO hired an independent contractor to identify critical skills for RAIO officers, develop strategies to deliver training content, and support the development of new officer exams.[103] However, the exercise was a one-time effort, not an ongoing mechanism. As of April 2015, RAIO and Asylum Division officials stated that they collect feedback from new asylum officers immediately following each basic training course using an online survey collection tool. Asylum officers are encouraged to fill out a questionnaire related to the course and the instructor after each basic training module. At the conclusion of distance and residential training, RAIO officials compile the feedback and discuss ways to improve future sessions. However, both Asylum Division and RAIO officials stated that they review survey results as they are collected after each session rather than tracking trends across multiple classes of participants. Furthermore, asylum officers cannot use this feedback mechanism once they return to their asylum offices and begin adjudicating cases. According to RAIO officials, in June 2015, RAIO began developing a new post-training survey to assess the effectiveness of basic training for new officers. As of September 2015, the survey instrument is in draft form and undergoing internal review. RAIO officials said they plan to survey participants from the calendar year 2015 basic training program, and may include participants who attended basic training prior to 2015. However, RAIO officials stated that, like the online surveys following basic training modules, this survey will be limited to new asylum officers.

Asylum Division officials stated that they collect information on training needs through monthly calls with Training Officers in each asylum office, as well as a recently implemented Quality Workplace Initiative to allow asylum officers to provide feedback within asylum offices on any topic or issue. However, the Asylum Division does not request information on training needs from the officers themselves on a regular basis and has not formally analyzed officer training needs over time. Further, the Asylum Division does not specifically solicit feedback on training needs through the Quality Workplace Initiative. Asylum Division officials stated that they previously collected feedback from new officers several months after they returned from basic training, but they discontinued this practice because of low response rates and a lack of resources. Asylum Division officials stated that it is difficult to devote resources to assessing the training needs of existing asylum officers when much of the Asylum Division's training resources are devoted to training newly hired asylum officers. GAO's *Guide for Strategic Training and Development Efforts in the Federal Government* states that evaluating training can aid decision makers in managing scarce resources and provide agencies information to systematically track the cost and delivery of training and assess the benefits of these efforts.[104] Further, *Standards for Internal Control in the Federal Government* states that effective management of an organization's workforce includes relevant training and that management must continually assess and evaluate its internal control activities to ensure that the control activities being used are effective and updated when necessary.[105]

During our interviews with asylum officers and RAIO and Asylum Division officials, the perspectives regarding the effectiveness of the training program varied. Both RAIO and Asylum Division officials said that the asylum officer basic training was sufficient and thoroughly prepared officers to adjudicate cases; however, officers we spoke with in six of eight asylum offices stated that the basic training was insufficient.[106] Specifically, asylum officer perspectives on the sufficiency of their training on credibility differed from those of RAIO and Asylum Division officials. According to Asylum Division officials, training on credibility provides information to asylum officers on how, for example, they can ask questions during interviews to determine whether an applicant's claim is credible. Suspected contradictions in an applicant's testimony may indicate credibility concerns or fraud. Therefore, officials stated that ongoing training related to credibility is crucial for new officers. However, asylum officers we spoke with in seven of the eight asylum offices stated that USCIS's credibility training is insufficient for asylum officers.[107] Both RAIO and Asylum Division basic training includes modules on credibility; however, as of June 2015, the Asylum Division's credibility training materials were under revision. Although the draft credibility training materials we analyzed discussed legal standards of credibility and case law analysis, the lesson plan contained blank sections, and unlike other RAIO and Asylum Division training materials, did not include sample decisions, or memos asylum officers can use to document such concerns. According to our analysis of the weekly training reports, 11 of 408 training sessions were reported as being dedicated to credibility determinations.

The *Guide for Strategic Training and Development Efforts in the Federal Government* states that agencies should be able to evaluate training and development programs and demonstrate how these efforts help develop employees and improve the agencies' performance.[108] Additionally, because the evaluation of training and development programs can aid decision makers in managing scarce resources, our guide notes the importance of agencies' need for developing evaluation processes that systematically track the cost and delivery of training and development efforts and assess the benefits of these efforts. USCIS does not have mechanisms in place to allow asylum officers to provide feedback about training needs after they begin adjudicating cases, making it difficult for Asylum Division headquarters officials to regularly obtain perspectives from asylum officers and supervisory officers about asylum officer training. In addition, asylum officers at one asylum office we spoke with said that a training feedback loop would improve training for asylum officers by allowing them to make suggestions for future training. Asylum officers within that office said they have made training requests to supervisors in the past, but did not see any follow-up or improvements as a result of their suggestions. Developing and implementing a mechanism to regularly collect feedback from asylum officers and supervisory asylum officers on their training needs would provide USCIS with insights to help the agency better evaluate its training program, and enhance the training courses based on asylum officer feedback.

## USCIS Does Not Have Readily Available Data on Asylum Officer Attrition

According to the Chief of the Asylum Division and other senior division officials, it has been difficult for USCIS to retain asylum officers because of the challenging nature of the position and the variety of other career opportunities available to asylum officers; however, USCIS does not systematically collect or analyze attrition data for asylum officers—a key component of strategic workforce planning. Asylum Division officials told us they use DHS's staffing database, the Table of Organization Position System (TOPS), to track net asylum officer staffing changes for each fiscal year.[109] However, these officials stated that this database does not capture comprehensive asylum officer attrition rates. For example, Asylum Division officials stated that TOPS does not track total hiring for each position type within the division and does not record departures from the asylum officer position when officers transfer within USCIS. Asylum Division officials also stated that they collect information monthly from each asylum office on all personnel changes, including new hires, transfers, and departures. However, Asylum Division officials told us that they do not collect these data in a systematic manner and rely on asylum offices to manually collect and report them to headquarters. In April 2015, we requested asylum officer attrition data from the Asylum Division for fiscal years 2010 through 2014. At the conclusion of our audit work, in September 2015, the Asylum Division provided updated attrition data that officials stated were reliable. These data differed significantly from the initial data provided in August 2015. Asylum

Division officials stated that they had compiled these data by manually reviewing all personnel changes in the Asylum Division for fiscal years 2010 through 2014, a process that was labor-intensive and required several weeks to complete.

Asylum officers and supervisory asylum officers we interviewed stated that, from their perspectives, attrition is high among asylum officers and this poses several challenges in effectively adjudicating asylum applications. For example, they stated that attrition has increased time pressures on each officer as asylum officers resign or transfer out of the Asylum Division. Officers we interviewed at all eight asylum offices told us that they face pressure from time constraints, which affects their ability to devote time to detecting fraud in asylum applications. In addition, according to senior Asylum Division officials, attrition requires USCIS to hire new, inexperienced officers who are not as knowledgeable about how to detect asylum fraud as more experienced officers. Supervisory asylum officers we spoke with told us that fraud detection is a skill honed through experience, and that newer asylum officers hired as a result of increased attrition are less skilled at being able to detect fraud in asylum applications. Asylum Division officials told us that they have faced challenges because of attrition and are working to reduce attrition among asylum officers. For example, Asylum Division officials told us that they created a new "senior asylum officer" position in 2014 to provide greater opportunity for advancement and have worked to support staff through training and mentoring programs. However, without reliable attrition data, it is difficult for USCIS to assess the effectiveness of these efforts in retaining staff.

*Key Principles of Effective Strategic Workforce Planning* states that federal agencies should develop a strategic workforce plan that incorporates management, employee, and stakeholder input, and identifies critical skills and competencies needed to achieve programmatic goals.[110] Further, the strategic workforce plan should address gaps in the number of staff, ensure that administrative and educational requirements are supporting workforce planning strategies, and monitor and evaluate progress toward programmatic goals. Without reliable, readily-available attrition data, USCIS does not have the information needed to develop an effective workforce planning strategy to determine the number of staff needed to address the increase in affirmative asylum applications and the applications backlog.

## USCIS Could Enhance Its Quality Assurance Processes by Examining for Indicators of Fraud

USCIS has implemented some quality assurance procedures for asylum decisions that are designed to ensure asylum officers' decisions are legally sufficient. However, USCIS's random quality assurance reviews of asylum cases do not include examination of potential indicators of fraud in the case file. USCIS has a three-tiered framework for conducting quality reviews of asylum decisions.

- First, the Asylum Division requires a supervisory asylum officer to review every case file to assess whether the asylum officer's decision is supported by law and the asylum officer followed proper procedures. For fiscal year 2014, USCIS also released new guidelines for asylum officer performance evaluation, which specify that supervisory asylum officers are to evaluate and provide feedback on whether asylum officers appropriately referred fraud indicators to FDNS and submitted fraudulent documents to the Forensic Laboratory or for overseas verification.
- Second, the Asylum Division's Quality Assurance Branch requires that asylum offices submit certain types of cases to Asylum Division headquarters for review. According to Quality Assurance Branch officials, these reviews focus on sensitive asylum cases, such as cases involving complex issues of law or cases that could result in particularly negative outcomes if the applicant is improperly denied asylum, such as cases involving a juvenile. For example, as of July 2015, the Quality Assurance Branch requires asylum offices to submit to headquarters all cases for which the principal applicant is under 18 years of age and the officer had decided not to grant asylum.[111] Our review of Quality Assurance Branch data found that, from fiscal years 2010 through 2014, the Quality Assurance Branch reviewed 5,696 applications. The most common type of application reviewed (3,213) involved juvenile applicants. The next most common reviews were of applications granted by an asylum officer for applicants from a country contiguous to the United States (Canada or Mexico) that relate to "novel" legal issues or criminal activity by the applicant in the United States or abroad (829 cases), applications that USCIS determined are likely to be publicized (425), and applications involving potential national security or terrorism risks (414).

- Third, each asylum office has a Training Officer, who, in addition to developing weekly training for asylum officers, also plays a quality assurance role. However, the extent of this function varies from office to office. Training Officers in six of the eight asylum offices stated that they generally review cases that are required to be submitted for headquarters review. None of the Training Officers we interviewed conducted random reviews of asylum applications and none reviewed applications for indicators of fraud, according to our interviews and observations.

In 2008, we reported that although the Asylum Division had a quality review framework to ensure the quality and consistency of asylum decisions, local quality assurance reviews did not always occur.[112] We recommended that USCIS develop a plan to more fully implement its quality review framework to, among other things, ensure that a sample of decisions was reviewed for quality and consistency. DHS concurred with the recommendation and, in response, in April 2009, the Asylum Division developed a program plan for reviewing a sample of asylum officers' decisions and subsequently piloted the materials it developed for implementing the program. Over a 2-year period in 2012 and 2013, the RAIO Directorate reviewed a sample of decisions from each of the eight offices. Since that time, USCIS has not reviewed further samples of asylum decisions because it is still implementing the action items that resulted from the previous review and because RAIO plans to study credible fear in its next review. RAIO officials told us they tentatively plan to conduct another review of a random sample of affirmative asylum cases in 2017.

However, USCIS's random quality assurance reviews of asylum applications do not include examination for fraud or fraud indicators. RAIO's 2012-2013 random review of asylum decisions did not include fraud because, according to RAIO officials, asylum officers should have referred any cases with fraud indicators to FDNS. The Asylum Division's reviews of specific types of asylum applications are not random and do not include a review for fraud indicators. Asylum Division officials told us that they do not conduct random reviews of all asylum cases because they have already implemented 100 percent supervisory review of asylum decisions in the field. Furthermore, the Asylum Division's review does not include a review for fraud indicators because, according to Asylum Division officials, fraud is not a component of legal sufficiency in asylum decisions. The Fraud Framework states that ongoing monitoring and periodic evaluation provide assurances to managers that they are achieving the objectives of fraud prevention, detection, and response. For instance, monitoring and evaluation activities can support managers' decisions about allocating resources and can help managers to demonstrate their commitment to effectively managing fraud risks. Although supervisory review is an important step in fraud detection and quality assurance, it does not position USCIS to ensure quality and consistency across supervisors and asylum offices, does not provide insight into quality concerns across the Asylum Division, and does not allow USCIS to evaluate whether supervisors are reviewing cases for fraud appropriately. Given USCIS's plans to conduct future random reviews of asylum applications, including an examination of possible fraud indicators in such reviews would help strengthen USCIS's oversight of officers' adjudication of asylum applications and supervisory asylum officers' reviews of the officers' adjudications. Random reviews for fraud would also help USCIS evaluate how effectively supervisory asylum officers are implementing the new fiscal year 2014 performance evaluation guidelines for addressing fraud.

## DHS AND DOJ HAVE IMPLEMENTED MECHANISMS TO ADDRESS IDENTIFIED FRAUD, BUT USE OF THESE MECHANISMS HAS BEEN LIMITED

### DHS and DOJ Rarely Pursue Criminal Penalties or Discipline Attorneys for Fraud

#### *Criminal Penalties*

Law enforcement agencies can pursue criminal charges against individuals who commit asylum fraud; however, according to an official from the Executive Office for U.S. Attorneys, individual asylees who commit asylum fraud may be subject to removal proceedings, but are not generally criminally prosecuted. Under the terms of a memorandum of agreement between USCIS and ICE, HSI has the right of first refusal to investigate all FDNS fraud referrals. However, FDNS immigration officers we interviewed in six of eight asylum offices reported that HSI rarely accepts asylum fraud referrals from FDNS, or that HSI accepts asylum fraud referrals and then does not pursue them or closes them without further investigation.[113] In four of the eight asylum offices, FDNS immigration officers referred 0 or 1 asylum fraud cases to HSI from fiscal years 2010 to 2014.[114] In one asylum office, FDNS immigration officers reported that HSI had not accepted a referral from FDNS in the previous 2 years, and that the U.S. Attorney's Office, which is responsible for prosecuting asylum fraud cases, does not generally accept asylum fraud referrals. The understanding of these FDNS officers was that the U.S. Attorney's Office in that district prefers to have at least 100 asylum applicants connected to an asylum fraud case before the office will consider prosecution. According to FDNS officials, fraud cases associated with 100 or more asylum applicants provide for sentencing enhancements, which is one of the factors that influence the willingness of HSI and U.S. Attorney's Offices to accept a case. In another asylum office, FDNS immigration officers reported that HSI had not accepted an asylum fraud case for investigation since 2010. From fiscal years 2010 to 2014, FDNS immigration officers working in asylum offices referred 40 cases to HSI; however, as discussed above, FDNS cannot determine how many of these cases involved asylum fraud. In fiscal year 2014, HSI initiated 37 asylum fraud investigations, which resulted in 7 criminal arrests, 6 indictments, and 4 convictions.

ICE headquarters officials stated that criminal investigations for asylum fraud are more likely to be brought against attorneys, preparers, and interpreters who perpetrate large-scale asylum fraud than against individuals. For example, in April 2014, an immigration consultant who was linked by HSI to more than 800 asylum applications filed since 2000 in the Los Angeles Asylum Office was sentenced to 4.5 years in federal prison after pleading guilty to conspiracy, immigration document fraud, and aggravated identity theft. HSI began investigating this individual's business in 2009. HSI agents in all four of the locations we visited stated that they face challenges in investigating asylum fraud cases, such as competing priorities, confidentiality restrictions, and low interest from the U.S. Attorney's Offices that prosecute these immigration-related criminal cases. The FBI has also pursued asylum fraud investigations such as Operation Fiction Writer; according to FDNS officials, the asylum office sent repeated referrals to HSI about the asylum fraud ring associated with Operation Fiction Writer from 2005 to 2009. In 2009, HSI requested that the asylum office stop sending it information about Operation Fiction Writer, at which time the asylum office began working with the FBI to pursue the case. As of March 2014, 30 individuals had been charged in connection with Operation Fiction Writer. According to HSI field office officials, asylum fraud prosecutions are time and labor-intensive and typically do not result in lengthy prison sentences; as a result, both HSI and the U.S. Attorney's Office tend to focus on large-scale asylum fraud rings, such as those involving attorneys, preparers, and interpreters, rather than individual applicants. Because HSI does not prioritize investigations of single instances of asylum fraud, FDNS immigration officers we interviewed in seven of the eight asylum offices stated that they generally do not submit single-scope cases, in which only one individual is implicated in the fraudulent activity, to HSI.[115]

### *Attorney Discipline and Disbarment*

EOIR's Disciplinary Counsel can pursue a variety of penalties against attorneys who perpetrate asylum fraud in immigration courts.[116] However, as of June 2015, the EOIR Disciplinary Counsel has not taken action to publicly discipline any attorney for having committed immigration fraud who had not already been disbarred by his or her state bar authority. EOIR's Disciplinary Counsel has jurisdiction over the regulation of practitioners, who are private immigration attorneys, and other accredited representatives authorized to practice before the BIA and the immigration courts.[117] The Disciplinary Counsel investigates complaints about practitioners who may be engaging in criminal, unethical, or unprofessional conduct or in frivolous behavior before EOIR and takes disciplinary action, as appropriate. The Disciplinary Counsel works closely with EOIR's Fraud and Abuse Prevention Program, although the Disciplinary Counsel seeks to impose disciplinary sanctions against practitioners, while the Fraud and Abuse Prevention Program can refer cases to ICE HSI or other law enforcement agencies for criminal investigation. The Disciplinary Counsel may choose to resolve potential disciplinary issues prior to issuance of a Notice of Intent to Discipline by taking certain confidential actions against a practitioner. Such confidential discipline includes warning letters or informal admonitions for low-level misconduct or for first-time offenders. According to EOIR's Disciplinary Counsel, confidential discipline is intended to educate the lawyer about what he or she did wrong and how to improve conduct in the future. Public discipline imposed by the BIA includes a range of disciplinary actions, such as public censure, suspension, or disbarment. Disbarment, in which an attorney is prohibited from practicing law before EOIR's immigration courts and the BIA, is the most severe disciplinary sanction that the BIA can impose. According to the Disciplinary Counsel, to date, the Disciplinary Counsel has not prosecuted any original jurisdiction cases to the point of disbarment, which means that the Disciplinary Counsel has not requested disbarment for any attorneys who engaged in asylum fraud and who were not already disbarred by their state bar or a federal court. Disciplinary Counsel officials stated that they have not initiated any original jurisdiction disbarments against attorneys in part because of a lack of administrative resources to pursue such cases. The Disciplinary Counsel has completed reciprocal disciplinary cases, in which attorneys who may have engaged in fraud and have already been suspended or disbarred by their state bar or by a federal court, or who have been convicted of a crime, are also disbarred by EOIR. An attorney who has been disbarred by a state bar or a federal court is permitted to practice before the immigration courts until EOIR takes the proper reciprocal action.

## Circuit Court Rulings and Agency Priorities Play a Role in Recent Decreases in Asylum Terminations due to Fraud

Asylum terminations due to fraud are not common and have decreased in recent years. USCIS data indicate that USCIS terminated the asylum status of 374 individuals for fraud from fiscal years 2010 through 2014. In the same time period, USCIS granted asylum to 76,122 individuals. The number of USCIS asylum terminations for fraud has decreased in recent years, from 103 in fiscal year 2010 to 34 in fiscal year 2014. If a final order by an immigration judge or the BIA specifically finds that the individual knowingly filed a "frivolous" asylum application and the individual initially received a warning regarding the consequences of filing a frivolous application, then he or she will be barred from receiving future immigration benefits.[118]

Asylum Division officials attributed the decrease in asylum terminations due to fraud from fiscal year 2010 to fiscal year 2014 to several factors.[119] First, according to Asylum Division officials, USCIS made several policy changes in order to comply with two decisions of the United States Court of Appeals for the Ninth Circuit. In Robleto-Pastora v. Holder, the court noted the BIA's conclusion that asylees who adjust to LPR status no longer qualify as asylees and held, among other things, that an alien who has previously adjusted to LPR status retains that status unless he or she receives a final order of removal.[120] Accordingly, a former asylee who had already adjusted to LPR would no longer have asylum status to terminate.[121] According to Asylum Division officials, USCIS changed its policy nationwide in June 2012 and no longer pursues termination of asylum status for fraud after someone has adjusted to LPR.

In June 2012, USCIS developed a process, called Post Adjustment Eligibility Review, for addressing suspected fraud with respect to former asylees who have already adjusted to LPR. Under the Post Adjustment Eligibility Review process, an FDNS immigration officer reviews adverse information about the individual, documents a summary of findings, and forwards the file to an asylum officer. An asylum officer then reviews the evidence to determine whether sufficient evidence of fraud exists, and, if a preponderance of the evidence supports the finding of fraud, forwards the case to ICE OPLA, which reviews the case and determines whether the individual should be placed in removal proceedings.

Additionally, in *Nijjar v. Holder* (August 2012), the Ninth Circuit held that only the Attorney General has the authority to terminate asylum status because Congress did not confer authority to terminate asylum on DHS.[122] On the basis of this ruling, USCIS does not have the authority to terminate an individual's asylum status in the Ninth Circuit, which includes the Los Angeles and San Francisco asylum offices. Subsequently, in August 2012, the BIA noted that no other circuits currently share the Ninth Circuit's position that DHS lacks authority to terminate asylum, and the case before it arose within the Second Circuit; as a result, it would "only apply *Nijjar* within the jurisdiction of the Ninth Circuit."[123] Therefore, Asylum Division officials stated that USCIS applied the *Nijjar* ruling only in the asylum offices located within the Ninth Circuit—San Francisco and Los Angeles. Asylum Division officials stated that these two decisions in the Ninth Circuit resulted in a decrease in the number of terminations conducted by USCIS because, prior to these decisions, USCIS would pursue termination of the asylum status of individuals who had adjusted to LPR nationwide and was able to terminate asylum status in the Ninth Circuit.

Second, Asylum Division officials stated that increases in the number of affirmative asylum, credible fear, and reasonable fear applications in recent years have strained resources in the Asylum Division, the immigration courts, and ICE OPLA. Terminations are time and labor- intensive, according to Asylum Division officials, and there are fewer resources available to pursue them than in the past because of the increased asylum caseload. In seven of the eight asylum offices, asylum officers we spoke with stated that terminations are not a priority. [124]

Third, Asylum Division officials stated that individuals who lose their asylum status because of fraud generally would not fit within the Secretary of Homeland Security's enforcement priorities, making the likelihood very low that they would be removed from the United States after their asylum status has been terminated. DHS's enforcement and removal priorities focus on the removal of aliens who pose a threat to national security, border security, and public safety.[125]

On the basis of our analysis of USCIS, EOIR, and ICE Enforcement and Removal Operations data, we found that 14 of the 374 people who had their asylum status terminated for fraud from fiscal years 2010 through 2014 were indicated as having been removed from the country by ICE Enforcement and Removal Operations as of March 2015; 4 were granted voluntary departure; and 20 had been ordered removed by an immigration judge, but ICE had not yet removed them.

## USCIS Has Not Tracked Asylum Cases Pending Termination due to Fraud and Has Limited Goals for Terminations

USCIS has taken some steps to address asylum cases pending termination due to fraud but has not tracked these cases or established goals for completing termination cases. The Asylum Division receives information about potential asylum fraud from a variety of sources, including USCIS offices that adjudicate asylees' applications for other immigration benefits such as adjustment to LPR and naturalization, and information arising from criminal investigations into attorneys, preparers, and interpreters suspected of engaging in asylum fraud. After receiving such information, the asylum office with jurisdiction over the asylee's place of residence reviews the case to assess whether to pursue potentially terminating the individual's asylum status, and, if a preponderance of the evidence supports a finding of fraud, sends the asylee a Notice of Intent to Terminate and schedules a termination interview. However, the Asylum Division does not begin to track cases pending potential termination until the asylum office issues a Notice of Intent to Terminate. The implementation of asylum office procedures for addressing terminations across asylum offices varies. For example, in one office, asylum officers maintain hard copies of the files pending termination in a particular area of the office's file room. In another office, asylum officers maintained a spreadsheet of pending termination cases. In other offices, there is an asylum officer responsible for handling terminations, typically on a part-time basis. However, the Asylum Division does not track the number of cases that are pending review for potential termination across asylum offices, making it difficult for USCIS to know how many of such cases exist and are pending review. The Fraud Framework states that it is important for agencies to ensure that the response to fraud is prompt and consistently applied.[126] Moreover, the Fraud Framework states that monitoring response activities helps ensure that the response to identified fraud is prompt and consistently applied. Monitoring fraud response activities, such as tracking asylum cases pending termination due to fraud, could help the Asylum Division ensure that cases pending termination due to fraud are managed promptly and consistently. Asylum Division officials told us that they have identified a need for greater tracking of cases pending termination review to better address requests for the asylees' files from other USCIS offices. In May 2015, Asylum Division officials requested a modification to RAPS that would give asylum officers the capability to record that a case is pending review for termination. As of September 2015, Asylum Division officials stated that this modification would be released in November 2015.

In addition, the Asylum Division has limited goals or metrics for reviewing termination cases, such as goals or metrics for the completion of terminations. According to USCIS officials, USCIS faces progressively higher burdens of proof to address potential asylum fraud as the asylee receives additional immigration benefits, which requires more time and resources. In August 2015, the Asylum Division adopted a new target of 180 days for conducting initial termination reviews that applies solely for cases with pending applications for adjustment to LPR. [127] This goal is a positive step, but it addresses the subset of pending terminations for individuals with pending applications for adjustment to LPR and it applies only to initial termination reviews rather than termination completions.

Furthermore, asylees who have not applied for adjustment to LPR may be eligible to receive certain federal benefits, such as Supplemental Security Income, Supplemental Nutrition Assistance Program, Temporary Assistance for Needy Families, and Medicaid; the new 180-day target will not apply to these individuals unless and until they apply to adjust to LPR. Asylum Division officials stated that they periodically review the number of terminations pending review in each asylum office to assess staffing needs, and asylum offices may also choose to prioritize certain termination reviews, as needed. However, Asylum Division officials stated that the division has not adopted goals or metrics for the completion of terminations because termination proceedings are extremely labor- intensive and asylum offices have limited resources to allocate to terminations. Asylum Division officials also stated that terminations are not a priority for their officers given increases in their adjudicative case load of affirmative asylum, credible fear, and reasonable fear cases as well as the prioritization of certain time sensitive cases, such as those involving unaccompanied minors.

According to the Fraud Framework, the likelihood that individuals who engage in fraud will be identified and punished serves to deter others from engaging in fraudulent behavior. Timely reviews of potential asylum terminations can also help the Asylum Division use its resources more effectively because, according to Asylum Division and FDNS officials, USCIS faces progressively higher burdens to address potential asylum fraud as the asylee receives additional immigration benefits. USCIS's new 180-day target for conducting initial termination review for cases with pending applications to adjust to LPR is a positive step; however, developing and implementing timeliness goals for all pending termination reviews of asylees granted affirmative asylum would help USCIS to better identify the staffing resources needed to address the terminations workload and better utilize existing resources to address potential fraud before asylees adjust to LPR or receive other immigration or federal benefits.

## CONCLUSION

The U.S. asylum process is designed to protect those who legitimately fled persecution, affording them the opportunity to prove their eligibility and credibility. Adjudicating asylum cases is a challenging undertaking because asylum officers do not always have the means to determine which claims are authentic and which are fraudulent. With potentially serious consequences for asylum applicants if they are incorrectly denied asylum balanced against the importance of maintaining the integrity of the asylum system, asylum officers and immigration judges must make the best decisions they can within the constraints they face.

Both DHS and DOJ have established dedicated antifraud entities—an important leading practice for managing fraud risks—but these agencies have limited capability to detect and prevent asylum fraud and both agencies' efforts to date have focused on case-by-case fraud detection rather than more strategic, risk-based approaches. DHS and DOJ could be better positioned to assess and address fraud risks across their asylum processes. Specifically, regularly assessing fraud risks across asylum claims would help provide DHS and DOJ with reasonable assurance that their fraud prevention controls are effective and appropriately targeted to their fraud risks. Further, developing and implementing a mechanism to collect more complete and reliable data on FDNS's fraud detection activities, including the number of referrals that asylum officers submit to FDNS and the number of FDNS investigations that result in a finding of asylum fraud, would help USCIS officials determine how often FDNS officers have identified and pursued fraud indicators. In addition, identifying and implementing tools for identifying fraud patterns in asylum applications, such as automated analytic software and prescreening, would better position FDNS immigration officers to identify cases associated with particular asylum fraud rings and aid in the investigation and prosecution of the attorneys, preparers, and interpreters who perpetrate asylum fraud. Moreover, developing asylum- specific guidance on the fraud detection roles and responsibilities of FDNS immigration officers working in asylum offices would help those officers better use the tools that are available to them. By providing additional fraud training for asylum officers and regularly assessing asylum officer training needs, USCIS could better ensure that asylum officers have the training and skills needed to detect and address fraud indicators in the asylum applications they adjudicate. Additionally, including an examination of possible fraud indicators in future USCIS random reviews of asylum decisions would help strengthen USCIS's oversight of officers' adjudication of asylum applications and supervisory asylum officers' reviews of the those adjudications. Last, developing and implementing timeliness goals for all pending termination reviews of asylees granted affirmative asylum would help USCIS better utilize existing resources by addressing potential fraud before asylees adjust to LPR or receive other immigration or federal benefits.

## RECOMMENDATIONS FOR EXECUTIVE ACTION

To provide reasonable assurance that EOIR's fraud prevention controls are adequate, we recommend that the Attorney General direct EOIR to conduct regular fraud risk assessments across asylum claims in the immigration courts.

To provide reasonable assurance that USCIS's fraud prevention controls are adequate and effectively implemented, and ensure that asylum officers and FDNS immigration officers have the capacity to detect and prevent fraud, we recommend that the Secretary of Homeland Security direct USCIS to take the following ten actions:

- conduct regular fraud risk assessments across the affirmative asylum application process;
- develop and implement a mechanism to collect reliable data, such as the number of referrals to FDNS from asylum officers, about FDNS's efforts to combat asylum fraud;

- identify and implement tools that asylum officers and FDNS immigration officers can use to detect potential fraud patterns across affirmative asylum applications;
- require FDNS immigration officers to prescreen all asylum applications for indicators of fraud to the extent that it is cost-effective and feasible;
- develop asylum-specific guidance on the fraud detection roles and responsibilities of FDNS immigration officers working in asylum offices;
- develop and deliver additional training for asylum officers on asylum fraud;
- develop and implement a mechanism to regularly collect and incorporate feedback on training needs from asylum officers and supervisory asylum officers;
- develop and implement a method to collect reliable data on asylum officer attrition;
- include a review of potential fraud indicators in future random quality assurance reviews of asylum applications; and
- develop and implement timeliness goals for all pending termination reviews of affirmative asylum cases.

## AGENCY COMMENTS AND OUR EVALUATION

We provided a draft of this report to DOJ and DHS for their review and comment. DOJ did not provide official written comments to include in this report. However, in an e-mail received on November 12, 2015, a DOJ audit liaison official told us that DOJ concurred with our recommendation that the Executive Office for Immigration Review conduct regular fraud risk assessments across asylum claims in the immigration courts. DHS provided formal, written comments, which are summarized below. DOJ and DHS provided technical comments, which we incorporated as appropriate.

DHS concurred with our ten recommendations and described actions under way or planned to address them. With regard to our first recommendation that USCIS conduct regular fraud risk assessments, DHS indicated that the Asylum Division and RAIO FDNS plan to develop an assessment tool and implementation plan for completing regular fraud risk assessments of the affirmative asylum process, with the first assessment to be completed no later than the end of fiscal year 2017.

With regard to our second recommendation that USCIS develop and implement a mechanism to collect reliable data on FDNS's efforts to combat fraud, DHS noted that FDNS plans to update user guidance and training materials and conduct training to clarify FDNS-DS data entry rules for asylum fraud referrals, leads, and cases and plans to complete these efforts by the end of fiscal year 2016.

With regard to our third and fourth recommendations that USCIS identify and implement tools to detect fraud patterns across applications and require FDNS immigration officers to pre-screen all asylum applications for indicators of fraud, DHS noted that USCIS recently approved a fiscal year 2016 budget request for such tools and stated that the Asylum Division and FDNS are coordinating with the Office of Information Technology to develop requirements and identify tools for acquisition. As part of this acquisition process, the Asylum Division and RAIO FDNS are also discussing the acquisition of software that would aid FDNS immigration officers in prescreening all asylum cases. DHS also stated that the Chiefs of the Asylum Division plan to issue a joint memorandum and companion guidance for asylum offices that will establish the framework for a national prescreening program.

Regarding our fifth recommendation that USCIS develop asylum-specific guidance on roles and responsibilities for FDNS immigration officers working in asylum offices, DHS stated that USCIS plans to issue a memorandum to clarify its guidance on the fraud-related roles and responsibilities of FDNS officers working in asylum offices by the end of fiscal year 2016.

Regarding our sixth recommendation that DHS develop and deliver additional fraud training for asylum officers, DHS stated that the Asylum Division is in the process of finalizing an updated lesson plan about fraud in asylum claims to be ready for asylum officer training by the end of March 2016. DHS also stated that it would provide this training to its asylum officers by the end of fiscal year 2016. In commenting on our draft report, DHS also stated that the draft did not reflect all of the fraud training currently provided to new asylum officers. In response to this comment, we clarified our discussion of USCIS's existing fraud training for new officers. Specifically, we added additional details about the fraud- related training sessions USCIS delivers as part of RAIO and Asylum Division basic trainings.

Regarding our seventh recommendation that USCIS develop and implement a mechanism to regularly collect and incorporate feedback on training needs from asylum officers and supervisory asylum officers, DHS stated that USCIS is in the process of preparing a division survey to be delivered to officers and supervisors to gather feedback on training needs in fiscal year 2016, and stated that officers and supervisors will be surveyed on training no less than once every 2 years.

With regard to our eighth recommendation that DHS develop and implement a mechanism to collect reliable data on asylum officer attrition, DHS stated that, beginning in September 2015, the Asylum Division has expanded the scope and frequency of its tracking of asylum officer attrition data. DHS stated that, moving forward, the Asylum Division plans to update its data on asylum officer transfers, promotions, moves to other USCIS offices, moves to outside employment, and departures from the labor force on a biweekly basis and confirm the accuracy of those data through regular validation. Based on this information, DHS requested that we consider this recommendation closed. While these are positive steps toward addressing our recommendation, USCIS needs to demonstrate that it has implemented its plans to update and validate its asylum officer attrition data to fully address the intent of our recommendation.

Regarding our ninth recommendation that USCIS review for potential fraud indicators in future random quality assurance reviews of asylum applications, DHS stated that, in October 2015, the Asylum Division added a fraud-specific question to the Asylum Division quality assurance review checklist. DHS stated that this change will ensure asylum cases selected for Asylum Division quality assurance will be reviewed for fraud indicators to determine whether those indicators were properly identified, analyzed, and processed. Based on this information, DHS asked us to consider this recommendation closed. While DHS has taken positive initial steps toward addressing this recommendation, to fully address the intent of our recommendation, DHS needs to demonstrate the extent to which this change allows them to review for fraud indicators in a random sample of all asylum cases, rather than in only the specific categories of cases that the Asylum Division headquarters currently reviews. As we note in our report, the Asylum Division does not currently conduct random reviews of all asylum cases.

Regarding our tenth recommendation that DHS develop and implement timeliness goals for pending termination reviews, DHS stated that the Asylum Division plans to revise its case management system, RAPS, to improve tracking of termination processing. The Asylum Division then plans to analyze the resulting data to develop timeliness goals for termination cases by the end of fiscal year 2016 and plans to implement those goals during fiscal year 2017.

These and other actions that DHS indicated are planned or under way should help address the intent of our recommendations if implemented effectively. DHS also noted that judicial constraints imposed by *Nijjar v. Holder* (9th Cir. 2012) have foreclosed DHS's ability to terminate asylum status for fraud in the Ninth Circuit, and stated that a legislative change would be necessary to restore USCIS's authority to terminate asylum status in the first instance.

Rebecca Gambler
Director
Homeland Security and Justice

## APPENDIX I: OBJECTIVES, SCOPE, AND METHODOLOGY

Our objectives were to (1) describe what Department of Homeland Security (DHS) and Department of Justice (DOJ) data indicate about trends in the characteristics of asylum claims, (2) evaluate the extent to which DHS and DOJ have designed mechanisms to prevent and detect fraud in the asylum system, and (3) evaluate the extent to which DHS and DOJ have designed and implemented processes to address any fraud that has been identified in the asylum system.

To describe trends in the characteristics of asylum claims, we analyzed U.S. Citizenship and Immigration Services (USCIS) Refugee, Asylum, and Parole System (RAPS) data on asylum applications, adjudications, and grants by asylum offices nationwide for fiscal years 2010 through 2014.[128] In addition, we analyzed record-level data from RAPS for asylum applications adjudicated from fiscal years 2010 through fiscal year 2014. To assess the reliability of the RAPS data, we reviewed USCIS documents about the design of the RAPS system, completed data entry and duplicate record checks, and discussed the reliability of the data with USCIS officials. We also analyzed two reports issued by the Executive Office for Immigration Review's (EOIR) Office of Planning, Analysis, and Statistics from fiscal year 2010 through 2014—*Asylum Statistics* and *Statistics Yearbook* . These reports contain data about the characteristics of asylum applications adjudicated through the immigration courts in the period of our analysis. To assess the reliability of the data in EOIR's reports, we reviewed EOIR documentation about the management of EOIR cases and appeals and spoke with officials about how EOIR collects and monitors data. The EOIR Office of Planning, Analysis, and Statistics changed the methodology it used to compile EOIR statistics in the reports issued in fiscal year 2013, and data from previous fiscal years are not comparable with those reported in fiscal year 2013 and 2014 reports. As a result, we relied on the fiscal years 2013 and 2014 reports for our analyses. We determined that the USCIS and EOIR data about the characteristics of asylum claims were sufficiently reliable for the purposes of this report.

To evaluate the extent to which DHS and DOJ have designed mechanisms to prevent and detect fraud in the asylum system, we identified the antifraud entities responsible for detecting and preventing asylum fraud within USCIS and EOIR and reviewed their asylum fraud data, policies and practices. We analyzed data from the Fraud Detection and National Security Directorate's (FDNS) case management system, FDNS Data System (FDNS-DS), about the number of benefit fraud cases associated with asylum applications that were opened from fiscal years 2010 to 2014 and the number of those cases in which FDNS found fraud. To assess the reliability of these data, we reviewed policies about how data are entered into FDNS-DS, such as the *Fraud Detection Standard Operating Procedures* and the FDNS Basic Training presentation that FDNS uses to introduce FDNS-DS to staff. We interviewed FDNS immigration officers and headquarters officials about their use of FDNS- DS and observed FDNS immigration officers using FDNS-DS. We discuss our findings about the reliability of the FDNS-DS data in this report. We also analyzed the extent to which the data captured in RAPS can be used to identify and detect asylum fraud. We compared FDNS immigration officers' reported use of the FDNS-DS system and FDNS-DS data capabilities with procedures in the *Fraud Detection Standard Operating Procedures* and standards in *Standards for Internal Control in the Federal Government.*[129]

To assess USCIS policies and procedures to prevent and detect fraud in the USCIS affirmative asylum process, we reviewed USCIS Asylum Division policy documents such as the *Affirmative Asylum Procedures Manual*, FDNS policy documents such as the *Fraud Detection Standard Operating Procedures and FDNS Field Priorities FY15*, and guidance such as the 2015 memorandum of agreement between FDNS and the Refugee, Asylum, and International Operations Directorate (RAIO) regarding the governance structure for FDNS. We reviewed Asylum Division workforce planning efforts to address asylum fraud and interviewed Asylum Division officials about attrition among asylum officers. We reviewed the Asylum Division Staffing Allocation Models, which officials stated were used to support Asylum Division workforce planning efforts, for fiscal years 2012 through 2014, the most recent years available, as well as the Staffing Allocation Model for fiscal year 2015. We also reviewed staffing levels for Asylum Offices, including asylum officer staffing and FDNS immigration officer staffing, from fiscal year 2010 to 2014 and compared actual staffing levels with estimates in the Staffing Allocation Models. We reviewed asylum officer attrition data, which USCIS compiled manually at our request. We compared Asylum Division workforce planning efforts with principles in GAO's *Key Principles for Effective Strategic Workforce Planning* to assess how USCIS workforce planning efforts align with the key principles.[130] We also reviewed USCIS quality assurance policy documents such as the *Quality Sampling Reference Guide and the Quality Handbook* and spoke with Asylum Division and RAIO officials about the extent to which these reference materials are used in asylum quality assurance. We reviewed documents associated with the random quality assurance reviews that RAIO conducted in each asylum office in 2012 and 2013, including the checklists used to evaluate asylum adjudications and the quality assurance results. We evaluated the extent to which these quality assurance reviews included reviews for fraud. We reviewed performance evaluation documents for asylum office staff, including asylum officers and supervisory officers, and examined the extent to which fraud detection efforts are reflected in staff performance evaluations, including the extent to which supervisory asylum officers evaluate the fraud detection efforts of asylum officers. We spoke with Asylum Division headquarters officials about ongoing Asylum Division headquarters quality assurance reviews of certain asylum adjudications. We reviewed past USCIS efforts to examine fraud in the USCIS asylum system and spoke with officials in the USCIS Office of Policy and Strategy about past efforts and plans for future efforts to examine asylum fraud. We compared these policy documents and their role in preventing and detecting asylum fraud with standards in GAO's *A Framework for Managing Fraud Risk s in Federal Programs* (Fraud Framework) and *Standards for Internal Control in the Federal Government.*[131] To learn about FDNS policies and procedures to detect and prevent asylum fraud, we reviewed FDNS guidance such as the Fraud Detection Standard Operating Procedures and training materials for FDNS immigration officers about asylum fraud as well as training materials for asylum officers about how to refer potential fraud to FDNS. We reviewed the extent to which asylum officers and FDNS immigration officers used other fraud detection tools such as overseas verifications and HSI's Forensic Laboratory. We compared USCIS efforts to prevent and detect fraud with leading practices in GAO's *Framework for Effective Fraud Risk Management*. We reviewed USCIS asylum officer basic training materials from RAIO and the Asylum Division, as well as training materials for FDNS immigration officers. We reviewed USCIS Asylum

Division quarterly training reports for fiscal year 2014 and used them to analyze the weekly training activities in each asylum office for each week of the reporting quarter. We compared RAIO and Asylum Division training materials with material in GAO's *Guide for Strategic Training and Development Efforts in the Federal Government.*[132]

We visited five of the eight asylum offices — Newark, New Jersey; New York, New York; Los Angeles, California; Houston, Texas; and Arlington, Virginia. We selected these offices for site visits based on a variety of factors, including their number of asylum officers, the number of asylum applications they receive, and geographic proximity to EOIR immigration courts. During our site visits, we visited immigration courts and observed asylum hearings in New York, Los Angeles, Houston, and Arlington. In addition, we interviewed approximately 11 ICE OPLA attorneys and 10 ICE HSI investigators in the New York, Los Angeles, Houston, and Arlington offices. In each asylum office, we observed asylum interviews and spoke with supervisory asylum officers, asylum officers, training officers, and FDNS immigration officers to obtain their perspectives on asylum fraud and the risk of asylum fraud. Although the results of our visits cannot be generalized to officers in all asylum offices or to all immigration courts, they provided first-hand observations on asylum adjudication practices and insights regarding policies and procedures to detect asylum fraud.

We conducted in-person interviews during our site visits and telephone interviews with supervisory asylum officers, asylum officers, training officers, and FDNS immigration officers in the remaining three asylum offices –Miami, Florida; Chicago, Illinois; and San Francisco, California. Across the eight asylum offices, we spoke with 35 supervisory asylum officers, 37 asylum officers, 24 FDNS immigration officers (including four supervisors), and 12 training officers.[133] We spoke with supervisory asylum officers, asylum officers, and FDNS immigration officers in all eight asylum offices about the tools and systems that they use to identify and detect asylum fraud and the roles of asylum officers and FDNS immigration officers in asylum fraud detection. We spoke with Asylum Division and RAIO headquarters officials about how asylum officers are trained to detect and prevent fraud, and how training needs are assessed. We also spoke with training officers in each of the eight asylum offices about how they develop and present training, as well as evaluate training needs. We spoke with Asylum Division and RAIO Performance Management and Planning officials about quality assurance mechanisms in the asylum program, such as 100 percent supervisory review of asylum officer decisions, and about the extent to which fraud detection and prevention is part of the Asylum Division quality assurance process.

The EOIR antifraud officer and the EOIR Fraud and Abuse Prevention Program are responsible for detecting and preventing asylum fraud within the immigration courts. We analyzed EOIR Fraud Abuse Prevention Program case files to determine the number of complaints received, number of case files opened, and number of asylum-related case files opened from fiscal year 2010 through fiscal year 2014.[134] We also reviewed 35 EOIR case files, which EOIR identified as being all cases associated with asylum fraud. During this review, EOIR classified two of these files as unauthorized practice of law rather than asylum fraud, and opted not to include a case file re-opened in fiscal year 2012 due to a prior case closure in fiscal year 2008.Two other case files were outside of the fiscal year 2010 through fiscal year 2014, which was the time period of our review. We reviewed EOIR's Fraud and Abuse Prevention Program guidance and policy documentation, including the regulation that established EOIR's antifraud officer position. We also reviewed the Immigration Judge Bench book, which includes tools, templates, and legal resources for immigration judges to use in their adjudications. We analyzed EOIR's fraud-related training materials for immigration judges, and spoke with the antifraud officer about the fraud detection and prevention activities associated with her role. While observing immigration court proceedings in New York City, Los Angeles, Houston, and Arlington, including asylum cases, we spoke with court administrators and immigration judges about asylum fraud.

To evaluate the extent to which DHS and DOJ have designed and implemented processes to address any fraud that has been identified in the asylum system, we analyzed Immigration and Customs Enforcement (ICE) Homeland Security Investigations (HSI) data on the number of asylum fraud indictments, criminal arrests, convictions, and administrative arrests as well as the number of asylum fraud cases initiated by HSI from fiscal year 2010 through fiscal year 2014. We also analyzed USCIS RAPS data to identify the number of individuals who have had their asylum status terminated because of fraud from fiscal years 2010 through 2014 and any trends in asylum terminations because of fraud over those years. We used ICE Enforcement and Removal Operations data to analyze the outcomes for individuals whose asylum status was terminated for fraud from fiscal years 2010 through 2014. We assessed the reliability of these data by reviewing documentation about how data were collected; interviewing knowledgeable agency officials about the data; and conducting electronic testing for missing data, outliers, and obvious errors. We determined that these data were sufficiently reliable for the purposes of analyzing the number of asylum terminations due to fraud and the outcome of those terminations. We reviewed USCIS policy documents related to asylum terminations, such as the *Affirmative Asylum Procedures Manual*, which details termination policy and procedures that are to be followed for asylum terminations. We also reviewed U.S. Circuit Court of Appeals decisions that were identified by Asylum Division officials as influencing how USCIS pursues asylum terminations due to fraud and USCIS policy documents related to asylum termination, such as the Post Adjustment Eligibility Review memo, that reflect USCIS policy changes made as a result of circuit court decisions. We visited five HSI locations – New York, New York; Washington, D.C.; Houston, Texas; Los Angeles, California; and Fairfax, Virginia —and interviewed officials about how they receive asylum fraud referrals and how they investigate allegations of asylum fraud. We interviewed officials from EOIR about mechanisms to address identified asylum fraud in the immigration courts and how those mechanisms are used, including disciplinary measures available to EOIR for attorneys and other practitioners who commit asylum fraud, and how frequently they are used. We interviewed officials in the eight USCIS asylum offices as well as Asylum Division officials to determine how USCIS handles cases with identified fraud, including cases in which fraud is identified after asylum has been granted, and how USCIS tracks, monitors, and adjudicates cases in which an individual's asylum status is pending termination for identified fraud. We compared USCIS and EOIR mechanisms to address identified asylum fraud and the frequency of their use with mechanisms in GAO's Fraud Framework to assess their likely effectiveness as a fraud deterrent.[135]

We conducted this performance audit from September 2014 to November 2015 in accordance with generally accepted government auditing standards. Those standards require that we plan and perform the audit to obtain sufficient, appropriate evidence to provide a reasonable basis for our findings and conclusions based on our audit objectives. We believe that the evidence obtained provides a reasonable basis for our findings and conclusions based on our audit objectives.

## APPENDIX II: FRAUD RISK ASSESSMENT PROCESS

GAO's *A Framework for Managing Fraud Risks in Federal Programs* notes that managers who effectively assess fraud risks attempt to fully consider the specific fraud risks the agency or program faces, analyze the potential likelihood and impact of fraud schemes, and then ultimately document prioritized fraud risks.[136] Moreover, managers can use the fraud risk assessment process to determine the extent to which controls may no longer be relevant or cost-effective. There is no universally accepted approach for conducting fraud risk assessments, since circumstances vary among programs; however, assessing fraud risks generally involves five actions, as noted in figure 8.

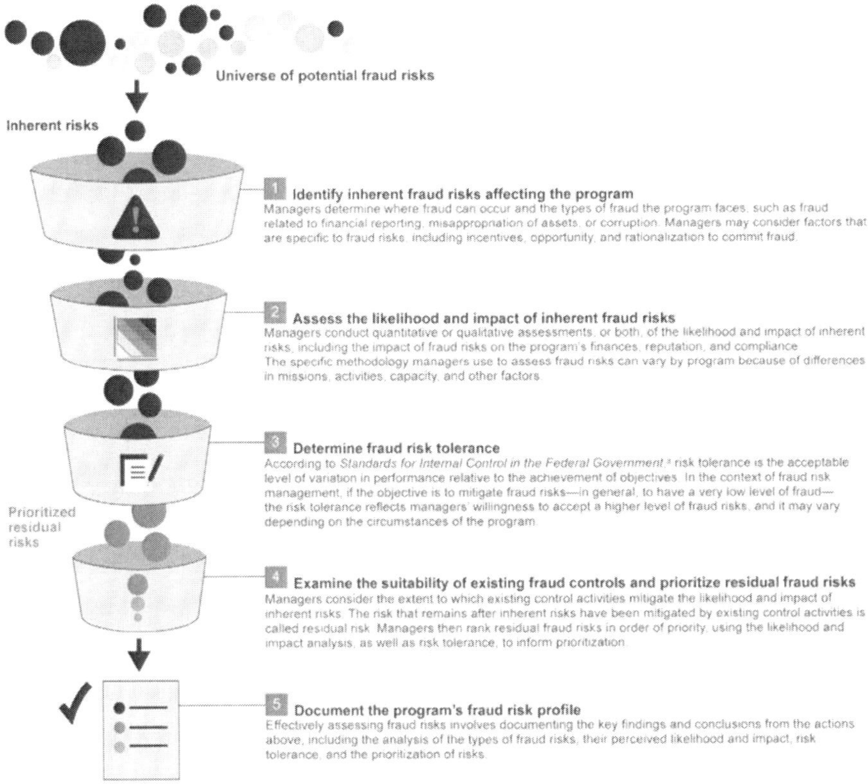


Source: GOA|GAO-16-50.

Figure 8. Key Elements of the Fraud Risk Assessment Process.

# End Notes

[1] The law s governing asylum protection were first established in statute with the passage of the Refugee Act of 1980, Pub. L. No. 96-212, tit. II, § 201, 94 Stat. 102, 102 06 (1980) (codified at 8 U.S.C. §§ 1101(a)(42), 1157-1159). The Refugee Act provided, for the first time, a U.S. refugee policy that stated that persecuted aliens who are present in the United States and who meet the definition of a refugee can apply for asylum protection in the United States. The legal standard f or a refugee and asylee are the same, but aliens must apply for refugee status from outside the United States and f or asylum status from within the United States. The final regulations implementing asylum and withholding of removal provisions of the Refugee Act of 1980 were issued in 1990.

[2] Office of the United Nations High Commissioner f or Refugees, *Guidelines on the Applicable Criteria and Standards relating to the Detention of Asylum-Seekers and Alternatives to Detention* (Geneva, Switzerland: 2012).

[3] For the purposes of this report, an asylum claim is defined as the prospective asylee's asylum application, as well as the totality of such asylum seeker's support for his or her application, to include written documentation, oral testimony, and any know n country conditions in the applicant's home country, among other supporting evidence.

[4] Subject to certain criteria, an individual who is granted asylum can remain in the United States and apply f or law ful permanent resident (LPR) status after 1 year. 8 U.S.C. §§ 1158(c), 1159(b).

[5] Within USCIS, the Refugee, Asylum, and International Operations Directorate (RAIO) is to provide, among other things, services for people who are fleeing oppression, persecution, or torture or f acing urgent humanitarian situations. RAIO is made up of three divisions: Refugee Affairs, Asylum, and International Operations.

[6] See 8 U.S.C. § 1158(a) (1), (2)(B), (D). Under 8 U.S.C. § 1158(a)(2)(E), the 1 year filing deadline does not apply to an unaccompanied alien child, which is a child who (1) has no law ful immigration status in the United States, (2) has not attained 18 years of age, and (3) has no parent or legal guardian in the United States or no parent or legal guardian in the United States available to provide care and physical custody. 6 U.S.C. § 279(g) (2).

[7] 8 C.F.R. § 208.14(c)(1) (where an applicant appears to be inadmissible or deportable, the asylum officer must refer the application to an immigration judge, together with the appropriate charging document).

[8] An alien making a defensive claim may have been placed in removal proceedings after having been stopped at the border without proper documentation, identified as present in the United States without valid status, or identified as potentially removable on one or more grounds, such as f or certain kinds of criminal convictions. Under 8 U.S.C. § 1158(b)(3)(C), USCIS asylum officers have initial jurisdiction of any asylum application filed by an unaccompanied alien child, even w here such child is in removal proceedings.

[9] The testimony of the applicant may be sufficient to sustain the burden of proof without corroboration, but only if the applicant satisfies the trier off act that the applicant's testimony is credible, is persuasive, and refers to specific f acts sufficient to demonstrate that the applicant is a refugee within the meaning of INA § 101(a)(42)(A) (8 U.S.C. § 1101(a)(42)(A)). A trier off act may determine that corroborating evidence should be provided in support of otherwise credible testimony, and such evidence must be provided unless the applicant does not have and cannot reasonably obtain it. See 8 U.S.C. § 1158(b)(1)(B)(i)-(ii).

[10] GAO, *U.S. Asylum System: Agencies Have Taken Actions to Help Ensure Quality in the Asylum Adjudication Process, but Challenges Remain*, GAO-08-935 (Washington, D.C.: Sept. 25, 2008).

[11] S. Rep. No. 113-198, at 132 (June 26, 2014). As part of the Senate Committee Report mandate, GAO was also required to review EOIR's asylum process. We have on going work in response to this mandate and expect to issue a report on that work in the summer of 2016.

[12] We selected fiscal year 2010 to fiscal year 2014 as our period of analysis as this w as the most recent 5-year period f or which data were available.

[13] U.S. Department of Justice, Executive Of f ice f or Immigration Review , *FY 2014 Statistics Yearbook*, prepared by the Office of Planning, Analysis, and Statistics (Falls Church, VA: March 2015).

[14] GAO, *Internal Control, Standards for Internal Control in the Federal Government*, GAO/AIMD-00-21.3. 1 (Washington, D.C.: November 1999), and *A Framework for Managing Fraud Risks in Federal Programs,* GAO-15-593SP (Washington D.C.: July 28, 2015). This framework is a comprehensive set of leading practices that serves as a guide f or program managers to use when developing efforts to combat fraud in a strategic, risk-based manner. GAO identified these leading practices through focus groups with antifraud professionals; interviews with government, private sector, and nonprofit antifraud experts; and a review of literature. We used the leading practices in this framework to assess USCIS and EOIR efforts because, as the framework states, it encompasses control activities to prevent, detect, and respond to fraud, as w ell as structures and environmental factors that influence or help managers achieve their objective to mitigate fraud risks; thus this framework is applicable to USCIS and EOIR efforts to address fraud in the asylum system.

[15] GAO, *Human Capital: Key Principles for Effective Strategic Workforce Planning*, GAO-04-39 (Washington, D.C.: Dec. 11, 2003). We developed these principles through our prior work on strategic human capital management, review of studies by leading workforce planning organizations, and interviews with federal agencies. We applied these principles to the USCIS Asylum Division, as these principles are designed to apply to any agency's human capital management and strategic workforce planning efforts.

[16] GAO, *Human Capital: A Guide for Assessing Strategic Training and Development Efforts in the Federal Government*, GAO-04-546G. (Washington, D.C.: March 2004). The guide summarizes elements of effective training programs and presents related questions on the components of the training and development process in f our broad, interrelated components: (1) planning and front-end analysis, (2) design and development, (3) implementation, and (4) evaluation. These criteria remain useful today because they are the most recent relevant guidance available to assess how agencies plan, design, implement, and evaluate effective federal training and development programs.

[17] The supervisory asylum officers, asylum officers, and FDNS immigration officers from whom we obtained input w ere not randomly selected from all officers in the 8 offices we interview ed. Officers were selected to participate in interview s on the basis of who was available during our planned site visits and who w as in a position to respond to our questions. Consequently, we consider the interview results to provide insights on asylum adjudication practices and procedures to detect asylum fraud, but these view s cannot be generalized to all supervisory asylum officers, asylum officers, and FDNS immigration officers in these offices or to the Asylum Division nationwide.

[18] We selected fiscal year 2010 to fiscal year 2014 as our period of analysis as this w as the most recent 5-year period f or which data were available.

[19] GAO-15-593SP.

[20] See 8 U.S.C. §§ 1101(a)(42)(A), 1158; 8 C.F.R. §§ 208.13, 1208.13. Certain categories of aliens are statutorily ineligible f or asylum even if they can demonstrate past persecution or a fear of persecution. The following individuals are ineligible to apply f or asylum: (1) those who have been in the United States more than 1 year without filing f or asylum, unless they can demonstrate changed or extraordinary circumstances; (2) those previously denied asylum unless they can show changed circumstances; and (3) those who may be removed to a third country w here they would have access to f air asylum procedures. See 8 U.S.C. § 1158(a)(2). USCIS and EOIR are prohibited from granting asylum to the following: (1)

persecutors of others and certain criminals; (2) those who are described in the terrorist grounds of inadmissibility or deportability, or are reasonably regarded as a danger to the security of the United States; and (3) individuals who w ere firmly resettled in a third country prior to coming to the United States. 8 U.S.C. § 1158(b)(2)(A). The 1 year deadline and "safe third country" exceptions to asylum filing eligibility do not apply to unaccompanied alien children. 8 U.S.C. § 1158(a)(2)(E).

[21] GAO, *U.S. Asylum System: Significant Variation Existed in Asylum Outcomes across Immigration Courts and Judges*, GAO-08-940 (Washington, D.C.: Sept. 25, 2008). See Pub. L. No. 109-13, div. B, tit. I, § 101(a)(3), 119 Stat. 231, 303 (codified at 8 U.S.C. § 1158(b)(1)(B)).

[22] 8 U.S.C. § 1158(b)(1)(B).

[23] See id. § 1158(b)(1)(B)(iii).

[24] Id.

[25] When qualifying family members of an asylee are in the United States but were not included in the asylum application or are outside the United States, the asylee may, within two years after asylum is granted, request accompanying or follow -to-join benefits f or such family members. See 8 U.S.C. § 1158(b)(3); 8 C.F.R. § 208.21.

[26] There are f our USCIS Service Centers. All accept asylum applications via mail and forward them to one of the eight asylum offices. The Service Centers are located in Texas, California, Nebraska, and Vermont.

[27] See 8 U.S.C. § 1158(a), (b), (d).

[28] The affirmative asylum process is nonadversarial in that no government official argues in opposition to the asylum applicant, and the asylum officer is to be a neutral decision maker. See 8 C.F.R. § 208.9 (Procedure f or interview before an asylum officer).

[29] 8 U.S.C. § 1159(b) (Statutory requirements f or an asylee to adjust to LPR).

[30] An applicant can apply f or several types of relief or protection from removal in one hearing. For example, we observed applicants applying f or asylum, withholding of removal, and United Nations Convention against Torture protection all at the same hearing. Withholding of removal under INA § 241(b)(3) prevents removal to a country w here there is a clear probability that the applicant's life or freedom would be threatened in that country based on race, religion, nationality, political opinion, or membership in a particular social group. See 8 U.S.C. § 1231(b)(3); 8 C.F.R. § 1208.16(b). Withholding or deferral of removal under the United Nations Convention against Torture prevents removal to a country w here the applicant establishes that it is more likely than not that he or she would be tortured if removed to such country. See 8 C.F.R. §§ 1208.16(c), 1208.17, 1208.18. The immigration judge can, and typically does, grant continuances f or additional master calendar hearings f or a variety of reasons, such as to allow time f or the individual to obtain representation or to obtain documents crucial to the case.

[31] 8 U.S.C. § 1158(c)(2); 8 C.F.R. §§ 208.24, 1208.24.

[32] See 8 U.S.C. §§ 1611, 1621, 1641(b).

[33] See 8 U.S.C. §§ 1612, 1613(b)(1)(B). Under 7 C.F.R. § 273.4(a)(6)(ii)(C), an asylee is eligible f or the Supplemental Nutrition Assistance Program, and is not subject to the requirement under 7 C.F.R. § 273.4(a)(6)(iii) that the alien be in qualified status f or 5 years. An asylee is generally only eligible for the Supplemental Security Income program during the seven year period beginning on the date he or she was granted asylum. See 8 U.S.C. § 1612(a)(2)(A). Asylees are also eligible for Medicaid until seven years after the date asylum is granted, at which point a state is authorized to determine the eligibility of an asylee f or Medicaid. See id. § 1612(b)(2)(A)(i). In addition, asylees are eligible f or the Temporary Assistance f or Needy Families and Social Services Block Grant programs; however, after the five year period beginning on the date asylum was granted, a state is authorized to determine the eligibility of an asylee for these programs. See id. § 1612(b)(2)(A)(ii).

[34] For example, asylees may be eligible for the Earned Income Tax Credit, a refundable credit available to low income workers, provided they meet specific Earned Income Tax Credit

requirements. See 26 U.S.C. § 32; Internal Revenue Service (IRS) Publication 519, *U.S. Tax Guide for Aliens*; and Publication 596, *Earned Income Credit (EIC)*.

[35] See 8 U.S.C. § 1158(c)(1)(B); 8 C.F.R. § 274a.12(a).

[36] See 8 U.S.C. § 1158(d)(2); 8 C.F.R. §§ 208.7(a)(1), (2), 274a.12(c), 274a.13(a)(2). According to the *Affirmative Asylum Procedures Manual,* an applicant can apply f or an EAD if his or her asylum application has been pending f or 150 days, not including any delays requested or caused by the applicant, or if the applicant has received a recommended approval of asylum. USCIS cannot issue an EAD until the asylum application has been pending 180 days or more. An applicant whose asylum application is denied within the 150 day period is not eligible to apply f or employment authorization. See 8 C.F.R. § 208.7(a)(1).

[37] See 8 U.S.C. § 1158(b)(3); 8 C.F.R. §§ 208.21, 1208.21.

[38] See INA § 274C, 8 U.S.C. § 1324c (civil penalties f or document fraud and criminal penalties f or failure to disclose role as document preparer). ICE's Benefit Fraud Unit defines document fraud, also known as identity fraud, as the manufacturing, counterfeiting, alteration, sale, and/or use of identity documents and other fraudulent documents to circumvent immigration laws or f or other criminal activity; and benefit fraud as the will ful misrepresentation of a material fact on a petition or application to gain an immigration benefit. Any alien who, by fraud or will fully misrepresenting a material f act, seeks to procure (or has sought to procure or has procured) a benefit under the INA, or who is subject of a final order f or violation of INA § 274C, is inadmissible and deportable. See 8 U.S.C. §§ 1182(a)(6)(C)(i), (F), 1227(a)(1)(A), (B), (3)(C)(i). There are also criminal penalties associated with immigration-related fraud under Title 18, U.S. Code. See, e.g., 18 U.S.C. §§ 1541-47.

[39] We developed this definition on the basis of an analysis of documentation from USCIS and EOIR, as well as through interview s with USCIS Asylum Division officials, USCIS FDNS officials, and EOIR officials who investigate allegations of asylum fraud.

[40] See 8 U.S.C. § 1158(c)(2); 8 C.F.R. §§ 208.24, 1208.24.

[41] Under 8 C.F.R. § 208.24(a), an asylum officer may terminate asylum granted under the jurisdiction of USCIS. Pursuant to 8 C.F.R. § 1208.24(f), "[a]liens who are currently in removal proceedings or were granted asylum by an Immigration Judge or the Board [of Immigration Appeals (BIA)] are under the jurisdiction of [EOIR]." See *Matter of A-S-J-*, 25 I. & N. Dec. 893, 897 (BIA 2012) (citing *Matter of K-A-*, 23 I. & N. Dec. 661, 665 (BIA 2004)).

[42] In *Nijjar v. Holder*, the Ninth Circuit Court of Appeals ruled that DHS does not have the authority to terminate asylum. 689 F.3d 1077, 1082, 1085-86 (9th Cir. 2012). Subsequently, in *Matter of A-S-J-*, the BIA stated that it would apply *Nijjar* only in the Ninth Circuit. 25 I. & N. Dec. at 894 n.2 (citing *Matter of E.W. Rodriguez*, 25 I. & N. Dec. 784, 788 (BIA 2012)). Therefore, USCIS lacks the authority to terminate an individual's asylum status in the Ninth Circuit.

[43] See 8 U.S.C. § 1158(c)(3); 8 C.F.R. §§ 208.22, 208.24(c), (e).

[44] See *Matter of A-S-J-*, 25 I. & N. Dec. at 896 (citing *Qureshi v. Holder*, 663 F.3d 778, 780-81 (5th Cir. 2011)). According to the BIA, "[a]n alien who timely filed an asylum application before the USCIS... is not time barred from filing the same asylum application before the Immigration Judge since the claim was timely made at the outset." Id. at 896 n.7. However, the BIA also cites, as a contrary position, the Ninth Circuit's decision in *Nijjar*. Id. The court in *Nijjar* stated that w here asylum status is terminated for fraud, a "second asylum application would ordinarily be time-barred, quite aside from whatever negative implication the fraud determination would have on the applicant's credibility in his second attempt to obtain asylum." *Nijjar*, 689 F.3d at 1081-82 & n.19. In *Matter of A-S-J-*, the BIA also noted that "[f]or different asylum claims, an alien who was already granted asylum status would not previously have had reason to file another asylum application[,] [and] [s]uch later-arising claims based on a different fear of harm would be evaluated under the regulations f

or changed and extraordinary circumstances." 25 I. & N. Dec. at 896 n.7. See 8 U.S.C. § 1158(a)(2)(D); 8 C.F.R. § 1208.4(a)(4), (5).

[45] See *Matter of A-S-J-*, 25 I. & N. Dec. at 896.

[46] 8 C.F.R. § 1208.24(f). Where an alien is in removal proceedings, DHS may serve a Notice of Intent to Terminate asylum and the immigration judge would have jurisdiction to decide the issue. *Matter of A-S-J-*, 25 I. & N. Dec. at 897. See 8 C.F.R. § 1208.24(e), (f).

[47] 8 C.F.R. §§ 208.24(a)(1), (f ), 1208.24(a)(1), (f). *Matter of A-S-J-*, 25 I. & N. Dec. at 896- 97; *Matter of P-S-H-*, 26 I. & N. Dec. 329 (BIA 2014).

[48] 8 U.S.C. § 1158(c)(3); 8 C.F.R. §§ 208.24(e), 1208.24(e).

[49] GAO-15-593SP.

[50] For the purposes of this report, references to the number of asylum applications include both principal applicants and their eligible dependents unless otherwise noted. Asylum decisions apply to the applicant and the applicant's dependents if included on the applicant's asylum application and the applicant established a qualifying relationship to them by a preponderance of evidence. An asylum applicant may include as dependents on the asylum application his or her spouse and unmarried children under the age of 21 who are present in the United States. Dependent applicants are not required to establish refugee status, and are not subject to the exceptions to asylum filing eligibility, but must prove that they are not barred from receiving asylum. See 8 C.F.R. §§ 208.21(a), 1208.21(a); 8 U.S.C. § 1158(b)(2)(A)(i)-(v).

[51] These defensive applications do not include applicants who applied affirmatively with USCIS and w ere ref erred to EOIR.

[52] Credible f ear cases involve individuals subject to expedited removal who express an intention to apply f or asylum or a fear of persecution or torture. Reasonable fear cases involve individuals subject to administrative removal or reinstated orders of removal who have expressed a fear of persecution or torture if removed. Credible and reasonable fear data represent individuals, not cases.

[53] See 8 U.S.C. § 1158(d)(5)(A)(iii); 8 C.F.R. § 208.7(a)(2) (an applicant failing, without good cause, to follow the requirements for fingerprint processing, would constitute delay not counted as part of the 180 day time period within which the asylum application is to be adjudicated).

[54] See 6 U.S.C. § 279(g)(2); 8 U.S.C. § 1158(b)(3)(C).

[55] GAO-15-593SP.

[56] FDNS does not have readily available data on the number of asylum fraud cases it has investigated, as we discuss later in this report.

[57] Authorities Delegated to the Director of the Executive Office for Immigration Review, and the Chief Immigration Judge, 72 Fed. Reg. 53,673, 53,675-76 (Sept. 20, 2007) (codified at 8 C.F.R. pts. 1003, 1240).

[58] See 8 C.F.R. § 1003.0(e)(2).

[59] According to EOIR officials, the Fraud Prevention Program revised its criteria f or opening a formal case file in calendar year 2010, an action that resulted in a decrease in the number of case files opened in in fiscal year 2010. The Fraud and Abuse Prevention Program no longer creates case files f or complaints or requests f or assistance that can be closed quickly with minimal investment in staff time.

[60] GAO-15-593SP.

[61] App. II provides additional information on the fraud risk assessment process.

[62] GAO-15-593SP.

[63] Although these applicants may have been connected to attorneys and preparers who were convicted on fraud-related charges, the number of these applications that w ere fraudulent is unknown.

[64] GAO, *Immigration Benefit Fraud: Focused Approach Is Needed to Address Problems,* GAO-02-66 (Washington, D.C.: Jan. 31, 2002).

[65] Booz Allen Hamilton, *An Evaluation of the Unpublished Report on the I-589 Asylum Benefit Fraud and Compliance Assessment,* Contract Number: HSSCCG-11- F-0053 9 (Sept. 18, 2012).

[66] See 8 U.S.C. § 1158(b)(1)(B)(ii) (an asylum applicant's credible testimony may be sufficient to sustain the burden of proof , without corroboration; however, the trier off act may require corroborating evidence in support of otherwise credible testimony, unless the applicant does not have such evidence and it cannot be reasonably obtained); 8 C.F.R. §§ 208.6, 1208.6 (with certain exceptions, information contained in or pertaining to any asylum application, or other records indicating that a specific alien has applied f or asylum shall not be disclosed to third parties).

[67] GAO/AIMD-00-21.3. 1.

[68] Pursuant to 8 U.S.C. §1158(b)(1)(B)(ii), uncorroborated testimony must be credible, persuasive, and refer to specific facts sufficient to demonstrate that the applicant is a refugee.

[69] The purpose of the asylum interview is to elicit all relevant and useful information bearing on the applicant's eligibility f or asylum. See 8 C.F.R. § 208.9(b).

[70] Asylum officers in the other office did not provide a response regarding granting asylum when fraud was suspected. Asylum officers must have legally sufficient evidence in support of a finding of fraud, in order to deny or terminate asylum on that basis. See 8 U.S.C. § 1158(b), (c)(2); 8 C.F.R. §§ 208.13, 208.14, 208.24; *Matter of Chawathe*, 25 I. & N. Dec. 369 (AAO 2010); *Matter of P-S-H-*, 26 I. & N. Dec. at 329 (BIA 2014).

[71] Immigration judges are authorized to respond to fraud in the immigration process on a case-by-case basis. 72 Fed. Reg. at 53,675 (citing *Ye v. U.S. Dep't of Justice*, 489 F.3d 517 (2d Cir. 2007)). An immigration judge may consider significant inter-proceeding similarities in making an adverse credibility determination, provided that certain procedural steps are undertaken to preserve fairness. *Matter of R-K-K-*, 26 I. & N. Dec. 658 (BIA 2015). In this case, the BIA stated that it was "not address[ing] what procedural protections are sufficient to offer an adequate opportunity to explain similarities between asylum applications absent a confidentiality waiver." Id. at 663 n.4.

[72] GAO-15-593SP.

[73] Although these individuals may have been connected to attorneys and preparers who were convicted on fraud-related charges, the number of these individuals who filed fraudulent asylum claims is unknown.

[74] We reviewed a total of 35 Fraud and Abuse Prevention Program case files provided by EOIR. During this review, EOIR classified 2 files as unauthorized practice of law rather than asylum fraud, and opted not to include a case file re-opened in fiscal year 2012 because of a prior case closure in fiscal year 2008.Tw o case files w ere outside of fiscal year 2010 through fiscal year 2014, which was the time period of our review.

[75] GAO-15-593SP.

[76] GAO-15-593SP.

[77] GAO-15-593SP.

[78] There is an exception to this policy f or classified cases or requests. If a request f or assistance refers to a classified case or requests classified content, that information cannot be entered into FDNS-DS.

[79] The crime of marriage fraud is to knowingly enter into a marriage f or the purpose of evading any provision of the immigration law s. 8 U.S.C. § 1325(c).

[80] GAO/AIMD-00-21.3.1.

[81] FDNS immigration officers in the five other asylum offices did not discuss this fraud detection practice.

[82] GAO-08-935.

[83] In their comments on a draft of this report, DHS stated that, as of November 2015, USCIS had approved funding to obtain such a capability in fiscal year 2016. However, the Asylum

Division and FDNS were still working to develop requirements and identify tools f or acquisition.

[84] GAO, *Immigration Benefits: Consistent Adherence to DHS's Acquisition Policy Could Help Improve Transformation Program Outcomes,* GAO-12-66 (Washington, D.C.: Nov. 22, 2011).

[85] GAO, *Immigration Benefits System: Better Informed Decision Making Needed on Transformation Program,* GAO-15-415 (Washington, D.C.: May 18, 2015).

[86] GAO-15-415. We recommended, among other things, that to improve governance of its Transformation Program, DHS should ensure that its Acquisition Review Board is effectively monitoring the program's performance and progress toward a predefined cost and schedule and relying on complete and accurate program data to review the performance of the program against stated expectations. DHS concurred with these recommendations and identified planned actions to address them, such as approving a rebaseline of cost, schedule, and performance expectations for the remainder of program.

[87] GAO-15-593SP.

[88] Asylum officers in the remaining two asylum offices did not comment about whether prescreening was helpful.

[89] Pub. L. No. 109-13, div. B, tit. I, § 101(a)(3), 119 Stat. at 303 (codified at 8 U.S.C. § 1158(b)(1)(B)(ii)).

[90] See 8 C.F.R. § 208.9(d).

[91] Supervisory asylum officers in the other three asylum offices did not comment about reinterview practices.

[92] In comments on a draft of this report, the FDNS Branch Chief for RAIO stated that one additional office began prescreening applications in October 2015.

[93] GAO-15-593SP.

[94] FDNS immigration officers in the other asylum office stated that the limited guidance allow s them flexibility to focus on areas of need in that office.

[95] FDNS immigration officers in the other asylum office did not comment about whether they submit single-scheme cases to HSI.

[96] FDNS immigration officers in the five other asylum offices did not specifically discuss FDNS guidance on site visits.

[97] GAO/AIMD-00-21.3.1.

[98] GAO-15-593SP.

[99] With regard to USCIS's fraud training, supervisory asylum officers and asylum officers in the other two offices did not provide a response.

[100] The staff meetings or a cancellation of a formal training category does not include office closures because of federal holidays or inclement weather.

[101] GAO-15-593SP.

[102] GAO-08-935.

[103] RAIO's three divisions include the Asylum Division, the Refugee Affairs Division, and the International Operations Division.

[104] GAO, *Human Capital: A Guide for Strategic Training and Development Efforts in the Federal Government,* GAO-04-546G (Washington, D.C.: March 2004).

[105] GAO/AIMD-00-21.3. 1.

[106] With regard to USCIS's basic training, one asylum office did not provide a response, and the other asylum office said that basic training was helpful.

[107] With regard to USCIS's credibility training, asylum officers in the other office did not provide a response.

[108] GAO-04-546G.

[109] According to Asylum Division officials, DHS's Office of the Chief Human Capital Officer maintains TOPS

[110] GAO-04-39.

[111] In September 2015, Asylum Division officials told us that they are working to transition to a random review of all cases involving juvenile principal applicants, including cases in which the officer decided to grant asylum.

[112] GAO-08-935.

[113] In the other two asylum offices, FDNS immigration officers stated that they have good relationships with HSI, but that HSI is constrained because, according to the FDNS immigration officers, prosecuting asylum fraud is a low priority for the U.S. Attorney's Office.

[114] In the other four asylum offices, there w ere 2, 3, 4, and 28 asylum fraud cases referred to HSI from fiscal year 2010 to 2014.

[115] FDNS immigration officers in the other asylum office did not comment about whether or not HSI accepts single-scope cases from the office. They stated that HSI typically accepts cases from their office, begins work on the cases, and then closes them without resolution.

[116] See 8 C.F.R. §§ 1003.101, 1003.104(c). Attorneys and representatives practicing before the BIA, the immigration courts, or DHS may be subject to the imposition of disciplinary sanctions in the public interest. See 8 C.F.R. §§ 292.3 (DHS disciplinary procedures), 1003.101 to 1003.109 (EOIR disciplinary procedures), 1292.3. While DHS and EOIR receive and investigate complaints of misconduct separately under their respective rules of professional conduct, Disciplinary Counsel for DHS or EOIR may initiate formal disciplinary proceedings before the BIA. Disciplinary Counsel for DHS or EOIR may, upon receipt of a disciplinary complaint or on their own initiative, perform preliminary inquiries, and where sufficient evidence of professional misconduct exists, will issue a Notice of Intent to Discipline and file such a notice with the BIA, charging a practitioner with professional misconduct as set forth in 8 C.F.R. § 1003.102, and seeking to impose disciplinary sanctions such as immediate suspension from practice (8 C.F.R. §§ 292.3(c), 1003.103). Where EOIR initiates disciplinary proceedings against a practitioner seeking to impose disciplinary sanctions such as immediate suspension from practice before EOIR, DHS may ask that such practitioner be similarly suspended from practice before DHS, and vice versa.

[117] In October 2015, EOIR issued a proposed rule which would, among other things, update the disciplinary process to make recognized organizations, in addition to accredited representatives, attorneys, and other practitioners, subject to sanctions for conduct that contravenes the public interest. See Recognition of Organizations and Accreditation of Non-Attorney Representatives, 80 Fed. Reg. 59,514, 59,515 (proposed Oct. 1, 2015) (to be codified at 8 C.F.R. pts. 1001, 1003, 1103, 1212, and 1292).

[118] See 8 U.S.C. § 1158(d)(4), (6). An asylum application is frivolous if any of its material elements is deliberately fabricated. Such finding shall be made only if the judge or BIA is satisfied that the applicant, during the course of the proceedings, has had sufficient opportunity to account for any discrepancies or implausible aspects of the claim. A finding that an alien filed a frivolous asylum application does not preclude him or her from seeking withholding of removal. See 8 C.F.R. §§ 208.20, 1208.20.

[119] According to the Program Manager for asylum terminations, the overall number of terminations has decreased from fiscal year 2010 to fiscal year 2014. However, the Program Manager also noted that termination for fraud has always been the most prevalent ground for which USCIS has terminated asylum status.

[120] *Robleto-Pastora v. Holder*, 591 F.3d 1051, 1056, 1060 (9th Cir. 2009, amend. Jan. 11, 2010). Subsequently, in *Matter of C-J-H-*, the BIA concluded that, like refugees, aliens w hose status was adjusted from asylee to LPR no longer qualify as asylees. 26 I. & N. Dec. 284, 285 (BIA 2014).

[121] Under INA § 246(a), rescission of adjustment of status may occur if, at any time within 5 years after adjustment, it appears that the person was not in fact eligible for such adjustment; however, nothing in INA § 246(a) requires that the alien's status be rescinded prior to commencement of removal proceedings under INA § 240, and an order of removal

issued by an immigration judge is sufficient to rescind the alien's status. See 8 U.S.C. §§ 1256(a), 1229a.

[122] 689 F.3d at 1082, 1085-86. Therefore, "[t]he regulations pursuant to which the Department of Homeland Security terminates asylum status, 8 C.F.R. § 208.24(a) and 8 C.F.R. § 1208.24(a), are *ultra vires* because the governing statute, 8 U.S.C. § 1158(c)(2), confers that authority exclusively on the Attorney General." Id. at 1085-86.

[123] *Matter of A-S-J-*, 25 I. & N. Dec. at 894 n.2. In this decision, the BIA determined that "[a]n Immigration Judge lacks jurisdiction to review the termination of an alien's asylum status by the Department of Homeland Security pursuant to 8 C.F.R. § 208.24(a)." Id. At 893.

[124] Asylum officers in the other asylum office estimated that, on average, the office completes two terminations per month.

[125] Jeh Johnson, *Policies for the Apprehension, Detention, and Removal of Undocumented Immigrants*, Washington, D.C. November 20, 2014.

[126] GAO-15-539SP.

[127] This target does not apply to Post Adjustment Eligibility Review cases, or to termination cases that are not pending adjustment to LPR.

[128] We selected fiscal years 2010 to 2014 as our period of analysis as this w as the most recent 5-year period for which data were available.

[129] GAO, *Internal Control, Standards for Internal Control in the Federal Government,* GAO/AIMD-00-21.3. 1 (Washington, D.C.: November 1999).

[130] GAO, *Human Capital: Key Principles for Effective Strategic Workforce Planning*, GAO-04-39 (Washington, D.C.: Dec. 11, 2003). We developed these principles through our prior work on strategic human capital management, review of studies by leading workforce planning organizations, and interviews with federal agencies. We applied these principles to the USCIS Asylum Division, as these principles are design to apply to any agency's human capital management and strategic workforce planning efforts.

[131] GAO, *A Framework for Managing Fraud Risks in Federal Programs,* GAO-15-593SP (Washington D.C.: July 28, 2015). This framework is a comprehensive set of leading practices that serve as a guide for program managers to use when developing efforts to combat fraud in a strategic, risk-based manner. GAO identified these leading practices through focus groups with antifraud professionals; interviews with government, private sector, and nonprofit antifraud experts; and a review of literature. We used the leading practices in this framework to assess USCIS and EOIR efforts because, as the framework states, it encompasses control activities to prevent, detect, and respond to fraud, as w ell as structures and environmental factors that influence or help managers achieve their objective to mitigate fraud risks; thus this framework is applicable to USCIS and EOIR efforts to address fraud in the asylum system. GAO/AIMD-00-21.3.1.

[132] GAO, *Human Capital: A Guide for Strategic Training and Development Efforts in the Federal Government*, GAO-04-546G. (Washington, D.C.: March 2004). The guide summarizes elements of effective training programs and presents related questions on the components of the training and development process in four broad, interrelated components: (1) planning and front-end analysis, (2) design and development, (3) implementation, and (4) evaluation. These criteria remain useful today because they are the most recent relevant guidance available to assess how agencies plan, design, implement, and evaluate effective federal training and development programs.

[133] The supervisory asylum officers, asylum officers, and FDNS immigration officers from whom we obtained input were not randomly selected from all officers in the 8 offices we interview ed. Officers were selected to participate in interview s on the basis of who was available during our planned site visits and who w as in a position to respond to our questions. Consequently, we consider the interview results to provide insights on asylum adjudication practices and procedures to detect asylum fraud, but these view s cannot be generalized to all supervisory asylum officers, asylum officers, and FDNS immigration officers in these offices or to the Asylum Division nationwide.

[134] We selected fiscal year 2010 to fiscal year 2014 as our period of analysis as this w as the most recent 5-year period for which data were available.

[135] GAO-15-593SP.

[136] GAO, *A Framework for Managing Fraud Risks in Federal Programs,* GAO-15-593SP (Washington D.C.: July 28, 2015).

In: The U.S. Asylum System
Editor: Eugene James Martin
ISBN: 978-1-63485-491-7


*Chapter 2*

# TESTIMONY OF LEON RODRIGUEZ, DIRECTOR, U.S. CITIZENSHIP AND IMMIGRATION SERVICES. HEARING ON "THE SYRIAN REFUGEE CRISIS AND ITS IMPACT ON THE SECURITY OF THE U.S. REFUGEE ADMISSIONS PROGRAM"*

Chairman Gowdy, Ranking Member Lofgren, and distinguished members of the Subcommittee, thank you for the opportunity to testify at today's hearing on the refugee admissions program, with particular emphasis on Fiscal Year 2016. As the Director of U.S. Citizenship and Immigration Services (USCIS), my team works in close partnership with colleagues at the Department of State's Bureau of Population, Refugees, and Migration (PRM), with other components within the Department of Homeland Security (DHS), and with colleagues in the law enforcement and intelligence communities to meet the U.S. Refugee Admissions Program's (USRAP) mission to offer resettlement opportunities to eligible refugees while safeguarding the integrity of the program and our national security.

As you know, the United States has a proud and long-standing tradition of offering protection, freedom, and opportunity to refugees from around the

* Footnote Citation Information: This is an edited, reformatted and augmented version of testimony presented November 19, 2015 before the House Judiciary Committee, Subcommittee on Immigration and Border Security.

world who live in fear of persecution and are often left to languish in difficult conditions of temporary asylum. USCIS remains dedicated to fulfilling this mission, in partnership with PRM, and continuing the United States' leadership role in humanitarian protection. An integral part of this mission is to ensure that refugee resettlement opportunities go to those who are eligible for such protection and who do not present a risk to the safety and security of our country. Accordingly, we are committed to deterring and detecting fraud among those seeking to resettle in the United States, and we continue to employ the highest security measures to protect against risks to our national security.

As the Director of USCIS, I can assure you that this commitment to our humanitarian and national security mandates is shared inside and outside of DHS. The refugee resettlement program has forged strong and deep relationships with colleagues in the law enforcement, national security, and intelligence communities and we continue to benefit enormously from their expertise, analysis, and collaboration. It simply would not be possible for us to support a resettlement program of the size and scope that the United States maintains without this critical interagency infrastructure.

My testimony today will describe USCIS's role in refugee resettlement generally, and I will discuss the screening measures and safeguards that have been developed by the USRAP and enhanced over time. While many of these enhancements were first deployed in connection with the Iraqi refugee resettlement program, they are now being applied more broadly to applicants of all nationalities, including Syrians who now represent a growing portion of our caseload.

## REFUGEE RESETTLEMENT CASE PROCESSING

As I mentioned above, the USRAP is a shared operational responsibility of the State Department and USCIS, among other agencies. The State Department is responsible for the overarching coordination and management of the USRAP, including the decision on which refugees around the world are granted access to the USRAP for resettlement consideration. As contemplated by section 207 of the Immigration and Nationality Act, this work is guided each year by a Presidential determination, which sets the refugee admissions ceiling following consultations with Congress. USCIS is responsible for conducting individual, in-person interviews with applicants to determine their eligibility for refugee status, including whether they meet the refugee definition and are otherwise admissible to the United States under U.S. law.

To maximize flexibility and program integrity, in 2005 USCIS created the Refugee Corps, a cadre of specially-trained USCIS officers who are dedicated to adjudicating applications for refugee status overseas. These officers are based in Washington, D.C., but they travel to multiple locations around the world. In addition, USCIS has a small number of officers posted at embassies overseas who conduct refugee adjudications, and we assign specially-trained officers from other programs – such as the Asylum Corps, Office of the Chief Counsel, and Administrative Appeals Office – to supplement the Refugee Corps. Using this model, USCIS has been able to respond to an increasingly diverse refugee admissions program, working in 64 countries in Fiscal Year (FY) 2015.

Recognizing that a well-trained cadre of officers is critical to protecting the integrity of the refugee process, we have focused our efforts on providing the highest quality training to our adjudicators. In addition to the basic training required of all USCIS officers, refugee officers receive five weeks of specialized training that includes comprehensive instruction on all aspects of the job, including refugee law, grounds of inadmissibility, fraud detection and prevention, security protocols, interviewing techniques, credibility analysis, and country conditions research. Before deploying overseas, officers also receive pre-departure training which focuses on the specific population that they will be interviewing. This includes information on the types of refugee claims that they are likely to encounter, detailed country of origin information, and updates on any fraud trends or security issues that have been identified. With the advent of large-scale processing of Iraqi applicants in 2007, USCIS officers who adjudicate Iraqi refugee applications began receiving additional two-day training on country-specific issues, including briefings from outside experts from the intelligence, policy, and academic communities. This training has since expanded to a one-week training in order to include Syria-specific topics as well.

In order to fully explore refugee claims and to identify any possible grounds of ineligibility, specially-trained USCIS officers conduct an in-person, in-depth interview of every principal refugee applicant. The officer assesses the credibility of the applicant and evaluates whether the applicant's testimony is consistent with known country conditions. These adjudicators also interview each accompanying family member age 14 and older to determine their admissibility to the United States. In addition, refugee applicants are subject to robust security screening protocols to identify potential fraud, criminal or national security issues. All refugee status determinations made by interviewing officers undergo supervisory review before a final decision is made. Refugee Affairs Division policy requires officers to submit certain categories of sensitive cases – including certain national security-related cases – to Refugee Affairs Division Headquarters to obtain concurrence prior to the issuance of a decision. This allows for Headquarters staff to conduct additional research, liaise with law enforcement or intelligence agencies, or consult with an outside expert before finalizing the decision.

## SECURITY CHECKS

Security checks are an integral part of the USRAP process for applicants of all nationalities, and coordinating these checks is a shared responsibility between the State Department and DHS. Refugee applicants are subject to the highest level of security checks, and a refugee applicant is not approved for travel until the results of all required security checks have been obtained and cleared.

All available biographic and biometric information is vetted against a broad array of law enforcement, intelligence community, and other relevant databases to help confirm a refugee applicant's identity, check for any criminal or other derogatory information, and identify information that could inform lines of questioning during the interview. Biographic checks against the State Department's Consular Lookout and Support System (CLASS) – which includes watchlist information – are initiated at the time of prescreening by the State Department's Resettlement Support Center (RSC) staff. In addition, the RSC request Security Advisory Opinions (SAOs) from the law enforcement and intelligence communities for those cases meeting certain criteria.

In the fall of 2008, USCIS launched a third biographic check with the National Counterterrorism Center (NCTC), which we now refer to as Interagency Checks or "IAC's." Initially the IAC was required only for Iraqi applicants, but the IAC is now required for all refugee applicants within a designated age range, regardless of nationality. In addition, expanded intelligence community support was added to the IAC process in July 2010. In 2015, all partners coordinated to launch IAC recurrent vetting. With recurrent vetting, any intervening derogatory information that is identified after the initial check has cleared but before the applicant has traveled to the United States will be shared with USCIS without the need for a subsequent query.

In addition to these biographic checks, biometric checks against three sets of data are coordinated by USCIS, using mobile fingerprint equipment and photographs which are typically collected at the time of the USCIS interview. These fingerprints are screened against the vast biometric holdings of the Federal Bureau of Investigation's Next Generation Identification system, and they are screened and enrolled in DHS's Automated Biometric Identification System (IDENT). Through IDENT, applicant fingerprints are screened not only against watchlist information, but also for previous immigration encounters in the United States and overseas – including, for example, cases in which the applicant previously applied for a visa at a U.S. embassy. Starting in 2007, USCIS began to work with the Department of Defense (DoD) to augment biometric screening by checking against the DoD Automated Biometric Identification System (ABIS). ABIS contains a variety of records, including fingerprint records captured in theatre in Iraq, and it is a valuable resource to identify a wide array of relevant information. Today, ABIS screening has been expanded to refugee applicants of all nationalities who fall within the prescribed age ranges.

In addition to the existing suite of biometric and biographic checks that are applied to refugees regardless of nationality, USCIS has instituted an additional layer of review for Syrian refugee applications, taking into account the myriad actors and dynamic nature of the conflict in Syria. Before being scheduled for interview by a USCIS officer in the field, Syrian cases are reviewed at USCIS headquarters by a Refugee Affairs Division officer. All cases that meet certain criteria are referred to the USCIS' Fraud Detection and National Security Directorate (FDNS) for additional review and research. FDNS conducts open-source and classified research on referred cases and synthesizes an assessment for use by the interviewing officer. This information provides case-specific context relating to country conditions and regional activity, and it is used by the interviewing officer to inform lines of inquiry related to the applicant's eligibility and credibility.

Throughout the review process of Syrian refugee applicants, FDNS engages with law enforcement and intelligence community members for assistance with identity verification, acquisition of additional information, or deconfliction to ensure USCIS activities will not adversely affect an ongoing law enforcement investigation. When FDNS identifies terrorism-related information, it makes the appropriate nominations or enhancements to the Terrorist Identities Datamart Environment (TIDE), using standard interagency watchlisting protocols. Additionally, USCIS drafts and disseminates reports to

U.S. law enforcement and intelligence agencies alerting the interagency to information that meets standing intelligence information requirements.

USCIS continues to work with DHS's Office of Intelligence and Analysis (I&A) and other intelligence community elements to identify options for new potential screening opportunities to enhance this already robust suite of checks. Finally, in addition to the checks that I have described, refugee applicants are subject to screening conducted by DHS colleagues at U.S. Customs and Border Protection's National Targeting Center-Passenger and the Transportation Security Administration's Secure Flight program prior to their admission to the United States, as is the case with all individuals traveling to the United States regardless of immigration program.

## THE REFUGEE ADMISSIONS PIPELINE

Given the wide geographic scope of the USRAP, including remote and sometimes dangerous locations, and the complexities of refugee resettlement processing, USCIS coordinates closely with PRM to develop a schedule for refugee interviews each quarter of the Fiscal Year. This yields a "pipeline" of refugee applicants who can be admitted to the United States, once all required security checks, medical examinations, and other pre-travel steps are completed.

In FY 2015, USCIS officers conducted refugee status interviews for applicants from 67 countries. The leading nationalities admitted to the United States were Burmese, Iraqis, and Somalis, as the multi-year program for Bhutanese nationals in Nepal continued its downward trend. Admissions from Africa continued their multiyear increase, notably including larger numbers of Congolese from the Great Lakes region of Africa.

Refugee processing operations in the Middle East, which have been primarily focused on Iraqi nationals since 2007, expanded to include a larger number of Syrian referrals from the United Nations High Commissioner for Refugees (UNHCR). As of late September 2015, the USRAP has received approximately 19,000 referrals of Syrian applicants from UNHCR, primarily in Turkey, Jordan, and Egypt. The USRAP continues to interview large numbers of Iraqi applicants in these same three locations, and has also resumed processing Iraqi nationals in Baghdad in spring 2015, after a break in operations since June 2014. USCIS was not able to work in Lebanon in FY 2015 – but for one exceptional, one-officer visit – due to space constraints at the embassy, where officers both live and work due to the security conditions.

In Fiscal Years 2013, 2014, and 2015, USCIS and the State Department have succeeded in meeting the annual refugee admissions ceiling of 70,000. This accomplishment reflects a worldwide commitment to refugee protection, as well as intense and committed efforts by all the interagency partners to improve, refine, and enhance the security vetting regime for refugee applicants, while maintaining its integrity and rigor. We will continue these interagency efforts to improve the quality and efficacy of the USRAP security screening regime, including progress toward more automated processes.

USCIS is prepared to work closely with the State Department and other interagency partners to support a larger refugee admissions program of 85,000 arrivals in FY 2016, including at least 10,000 Syrian refugees, while assiduously maintaining the integrity of the program and our national security.

I would be happy to answer your questions.

In: The U.S. Asylum System
Editor: Eugene James Martin
ISBN: 978-1-63485-491-7


*Chapter 3*

# STATEMENT OF MARK KRIKORIAN, EXECUTIVE DIRECTOR, CENTER FOR IMMIGRATION STUDIES. HEARING ON "THE SYRIAN REFUGEE CRISIS AND ITS IMPACT ON THE SECURITY OF THE U.S. REFUGEE ADMISSIONS PROGRAM"*

A wise man once said "The supreme function of statesmanship is to provide against preventable evils." Halting refugee resettlement from the Middle East would be just such an act of statesmanship.

The starting point of any policy debate is that the government of the United States has no responsibility to anyone but the citizens of the United States. As individuals delegated by the citizenry to deal with the business of the state, the president and members of Congress must necessarily put the interests of the American people before the interests of foreigners.

This means the United States government has no responsibility to refugees; they have no claim on it and no right to demand anything of it. If, nonetheless, we decide as a matter of policy to devote resources to humanitarian refugee protection (a policy decision which I personally support), then we should base our decision-making on two principles: 1) Such

* Footnote Citation Information: This is an edited, reformatted and augmented version of a statement presented November 19, 2015 before the House Judiciary Committee, Subcommittee on Immigration and Border Security.

policies must not pose a threat to the American people, and 2) the funds taken from the people through taxes for this purpose must be used to the maximum humanitarian effect.

Resettling Syrian refugees in the United States fails on both counts.

## 1. Security

There are two parts to the security challenge posed by refugee resettlement.

### A) Screening Cannot Be Done Adequately

During last weekend's debate among the Democratic presidential candidates, Hillary Clinton said that the United States should spend "whatever resources it takes" to properly screen Syrian refugees before they are resettled in the United States. This is a common-sense demand that virtually all Americans would agree with.

Officials have assured us that refugees are "are subject to more intensive security than any other type of traveler to the U.S. to protect against threats to our national security."[1] There is no reason to doubt this. The people in the departments of State and Homeland Security, and at the intelligence agencies they work with, are doing their best to protect our people from harm.

But this misses the point. The problem with trying to screen candidates for resettlement from Syria – or any other failed state, such as Somalia, Libya, Yemen, or Afghanistan – is not a lack of resources or commitment.

The problem is that it cannot be done.

Our vetting process is heavily oriented toward electronic checks of databases with biographical information and photos and fingerprints. But little information of that kind which could potentially disqualify a candidate for resettlement is available to us. DHS Secretary Jeh Johnson said last month that "one of the challenges that we'll have is that we're not going to know a whole lot about the individual refugees that come forward."[2] FBI Director James Comey confirmed this, telling a Senate panel last month, "The only thing we can query is information that we have. So, if we have no information on someone, they've never crossed our radar screen, they've never been a ripple in the pond, there will be no record of them there and so it will be challenging."

"Challenging" indeed. We sometimes imagine such information must be available for everybody abroad as it is here – birth certificates, death records, driver's licenses, school records, credit card charges, and all the other tracks we leave behind us as we navigate life in a modern, information-based society.

But such tracks are rare or nonexistent in much of the world even in the best of times. And in chaotic conditions like those of Syria – or Somali or Yemen or Libya or Afghanistan – what little existed of the information trail has gone up in smoke. As FBI Assistant Director Michael Steinbach told another committee of this House, "The concern in Syria is that we don't have systems in places on the ground to collect information to vet...You're talking about a country that is a failed state, that does not have any infrastructure, so to speak. So all of the datasets – the police, the intel services – that normally you would go to to seek information doesn't exist."

Our screening of refugees resembles the joke where a drunk searches for his lost keys under the streetlight because that's where the light is. The clearest statement of this came from Matthew Emrich, who's in charge of fraud detection at USCIS, when he told a Senate hearing that "We check everything that we are aware of within US government holdings." Because that's where the light is.

Databases are not the only tool used in such screening. Many candidates for resettlement will present documents purporting to show who they are. Mr. Emrich again: "In most cases, these individuals do have documents from Syria ... Our officers are trained in fraud detection."

Given the pervasive fraud in all the immigration categories overseen by USCIS, this may seem cold comfort, but ICE's Forensic Document Laboratory really does have unparalleled expertise. But the problem with relying on documents is twofold. First, many non-threatening refugees have fake documents too, and that's no bar in itself to being accepted for resettlement. There's good reason for this – people fleeing one faction or another of Syria's war of all against all may well have to lie about who they are to avoid capture or death. But even if we could identify every fake or altered document, how are we to distinguish the non-threatening document fraudster from the threatening one?

Second, the disintegration of Syria (and Libya, etc.) means that *legitimate* blank passports and other documents are circulating widely. Veteran immigration agent Dan Cadman explains: "This is because many Syrian government offices have been overrun in the chaos of war, leaving their trove of blank documents — passports, national identity cards, driver's licenses, etc. — behind for extremist groups and criminal gangs to take advantage of."[3]

ICE's Forensic Document Lab has genuine blanks of almost every country's passports for comparison, but that expertise doesn't help when false identities are inserted into these legitimate documents. Cadman again: "In such circumstances, there is no one that U.S. officers can turn to in order to verify the identity of the person who presents these facially legitimate documents."

The vulnerability of documents has been highlighted in Europe this year. Because of the preference given to Syrians, thousands of non-Syrian illegal aliens headed through Turkey to Europe have discarded their real passports and claimed to be Syrian, often presenting fraudulent documents. And one of the Paris attackers appears to have used just such a phony passport.

A final tool for screening refugees is personal interviews. It's true that experienced adjudicators can often sniff out liars and cheats from personal interaction. This works best as a supplement to other forms of screening, not as a substitute. But since those other forms are necessarily ineffective in conditions like those prevailing in the Middle East, pointing to interviews as a substitute is not encouraging. And let us not forget that the State Department's consular officers interview regular visa applicants, as well; but the presence of perhaps 5 million illegal aliens who were issued visas based on their promises made during interviews that they would go home suggests the limitations of this approach.

Finally, one would imagine that a strict vetting process would result in a relatively high rate of rejections. And yet, Barbara Strack, Chief of the USCIS Refugee Affairs Division, told the Senate hearing last month that more than 90 percent of Syrian candidates for resettlement were being approved. How stringent can the vetting of Syrian refugees really be when almost all of them are accepted?

## B) The Sea Within Which Terrorist Fish Swim

The broader security problem created by refugee admissions – or by large-scale immigration of any kind from societies with large numbers of terrorists – is that they establish and constantly refresh insular communities that serve as cover and incubators for terrorism. However unwittingly, such neighborhoods, and their mosques and other institutions, fit Mao's observation regarding the peasantry's role in China's war against the Japanese: "The people are like water and the army is like fish."

The Brussels neighborhood of Molenbeek, for instance, seems to have been the haven where the recent atrocities in Paris were planned and organized. Its predominantly North African-origin population is certainly mostly peaceful and unthreatening, but they nonetheless served as the water for the terrorist fish.

This applies in our own country as well. Charles E. Allen, DHS's chief intelligence officer at the time, told this House's Select Committee on Intelligence in 2007, "As previous attacks indicate, overseas extremists do not operate in a vacuum and are often linked with criminal and smuggling networks – usually connected with resident populations [in the U.S.] from their countries of origin."

One example of this phenomenon was the al Qaeda cell in the Yemeni enclave in Lackawanna, N.Y., outside Buffalo, which was broken up in 2002. Five of the six members were U.S.-born but raised in the immigrant neighborhood, which the local paper described this way:

> This is a piece of ethnic America where the Arabic-speaking Al-Jazeera television station is beamed in from Qatar through satellite dishes to Yemenite-American homes; where young children answer "Salaam" when the cell phone rings, while older children travel to the Middle East to meet their future husband or wife; where soccer moms don't seem to exist, and where girls don't get to play soccer – or, as some would say, football.[4]

No one of these factors, taken on its own, is especially remarkable in our diverse society. Even taken together, the kind of enclave they describe would be of little consequence if it were inhabited by, say, Amish or Hasidim, because those groups do not serve as "resident populations from their countries of origin" for violent extremist organizations like ISIS or al Qaeda or al Shabaab. But communities made up of refugees and immigrants from the Middle East do serve that purpose, however unwittingly – and cannot do otherwise.

The Somali community in Minneapolis is a prime example. Established through refugee resettlement, and continually expanded and refreshed by more resettlement (nearly 9,000 Somali refugees were admitted last year) as well as follow-on chain migration, it has been the source of dozens of recruits for al Shabaab and ISIS, and dozens more supporters. Just this summer, a Somali graduate of a Minnesota high school died fighting for ISIS in Syria. As the *Washington Times* noted, the refugee resettlement program "is having the unintended consequence of creating an enclave of immigrants with high unemployment that is both stressing the state's safety net and creating a rich pool of potential recruiting targets for Islamist terror groups."[5]

The combination of these two security vulnerabilities – the impossibility of vetting candidates for resettlement, plus the growth of domestic breeding grounds – is a big part of why the FBI has some 900 active investigations into domestic extremists, the vast majority related to ISIS.[6]

These investigations come in the wake of many examples of terrorism-related activities by refugees. (All parts of the immigration system have been exploited by terrorists, not just the refugee program; see, for instance, "How Militant Islamic Terrorists Entered and Remained in the United States, 1993-2001".[7]) For instance, two al Qaeda bomb makers were arrested in Kentucky after having been resettled as refugees. Nor are they likely the only ones; ABC News reported in 2013:

> Several dozen suspected terrorist bombmakers, including some believed to have targeted American troops, may have mistakenly been allowed to move to the United States as war refugees, according to FBI agents investigating the remnants of roadside bombs recovered from Iraq and Afghanistan.[8]

Other examples: An Uzbek refugee, who presumably underwent the stringent screening that the administration boasts of, was convicted in Idaho earlier this year on terrorism charges.[9] A number of Bosnian refugees, presumably also screened, were charged this year with sending money and weapons to Islamist groups in Syrian and Iraq.[10]

Some have suggested resettling only Christians and other religious minorities from Syria, because we could be fairly certain they would not be affiliated with ISIS or al Qaeda. And indeed, there currently appears to be a policy of discrimination *against* Christian refugees; Muslims are overrepresented among the Syrians whom we have resettled, perhaps in part because the UN selects the refugees for us from its camps, and Christian refugees fear going to the camps, lest the Muslim refugees kill them, as happened this spring when Muslim passengers on a smuggling boat in the Mediterranean threw 12 people overboard to their deaths because they were Christians.

There are two problems with this approach. First, how would we know if those claiming to be Christians really are? The church records of baptism and marriage that might be useful in that regard are likely either destroyed or inaccessible, and there's nothing to stop jihadists – or even non-terrorist Muslims – from studying up on enough of the high points of Christianity to pass muster. Many Chinese illegal aliens in the United States have successfully gotten asylum by pretending to be members of China's underground Catholic or Protestant churches. How much more successful would Syrian Muslims be in such a fraud, since they are probably already familiar with many of the outward manifestations of Christian practice, given the relatively large number of Christians living there before the civil war?

The second problem with admitting only religious minorities is that resettlement of refugees of any faith is a highly inefficient means of protecting refugees. That issue of effectiveness is subject of the next section.

## 2. Efficacy

In addition to the security threats that refugee resettlement poses, any effort to extend humanitarian assistance to refugees must consider how effective it will be. This question also has two facets.

### A) More Can Be Helped Abroad

Bringing refugees into our country makes us feel good about ourselves. Newspapers run heartwarming stories of overcoming adversity; churches embrace the objects of their charity; politicians wax nostalgic about their grandparents.

But the goal of refugee assistance is not to make us feel good. It is to assist as many people as possible with the resources available. And resettling a relative handful of them here to help us bask in our own righteousness means we are sacrificing the much larger number who could have been helped with the same resources.

The difference in cost is enormous. The Center for Immigration Studies has calculated that it costs twelve times as much to resettle a refugee in the United States as it does to care for the same refugee in the neighboring countries of first asylum, namely Turkey, Jordan, and Lebanon.[11] The five-year cost to American taxpayers of resettling a single Middle Eastern refugee in the United States is conservatively estimated to be more than $64,000, compared with U.N. figures that indicate it costs about $5,300 to provide for that same refugee for five years in his native region.

In other words, each refugee we bring to the United States means that eleven others are not being helped with that money. Faced with twelve drowning people, only a monster would send them a luxurious one-man boat rather than 12 life jackets. And yet, with the best of intentions, that is exactly what we are doing when we choose one lucky winner to resettle here.

Some will object that we can do both – relocate some refugees here and care for others in their native region. But money is not infinite. Every dollar the government spends is borrowed and will have to be paid back by our grandchildren. What's more, the U.N. estimates that there are 60 million refugees and internally displaced people around the world. Clearly, whatever amount we allocate to refugee protection will provide for only a fraction of the people in need.

Given these limitations on resources, I submit that it is wrong — morally wrong — to use those resources to resettle one refugee here when we could help 12 closer to their home.

There is little we can do to minimize the costs of resettling refugees. True, the private contractors the State Department pays to oversee the process are making a good living off of refugee resettlement, but reining them in won't make much difference. Most of the costs come from social services; according to the U.S. Department of Health and Human Services, more than 90 percent of refugees from the Middle East receive food stamps and nearly three-quarters are on Medicaid or some other taxpayer-funded health care.

This dependence on taxpayer handouts should come as no surprise. Refugees arrive destitute and often traumatized. They have little education (those from the Middle East have an average of only 10.5 years of schooling), which means that even if they find work, it will pay little. And because they're poor – almost all have incomes only slightly above the poverty line – they pay little in taxes.

Of course, we don't resettle refugees for economic reasons but for humanitarian ones. And since the goal is humanitarian, a wise steward must use his resources so that they generate the greatest humanitarian return. It's also true that refugees brought here will live better than those even in well-run refugee camps in the region. But the goal of refugee protection is to provide people adequate succor until they can return home, not maximize opportunity for a select few.

## B) Success of Refugee Protection Means People Go Home When Conflict Ends

A return home is the final measure of the success of any effort at refugee protection. The civil war in Syria, like a similar civil war in the 1970s and 1980s in neighboring Lebanon, eventually will come to an end. Any scheme of refugee protection should be designed with eventual repatriation in mind.

The most successful effort at returning refugees to their homes has been in Afghanistan. The UN reports that since 2002, nearly 6 million Afghan refugees have returned home from neighboring Pakistan and Iran (though many remain).[12]

While the UN doesn't track the statistic, the likelihood that refugees who've been resettled on the other side of the world will ever move back is small. It's not just that the physical distance is greater, though that is a factor. In addition, the acclimation to developed-world standards of living and norms of behavior and the assimilation of children into a new and radically different society make it vanishingly unlikely that those brought here, as opposed to those given succor in their own region, will ever choose to go home.

## 3. Conclusion

Congress has before it a variety of measures to address the Syrian refugee issue, including a temporary pause, a broader change in the refugee rules, and defunding proposals. As you consider how to proceed,

I would urge you to keep in mind these two points:

### 1) The Only Way to Reduce the Security Risk of Resettling Syrian Refugees (or Those from Somalia and Other Failed States) Is to Reduce the Number We Resettle

The government's obligation to make the most effective use of whatever tax monies we decide to devote to refugee protection compels a shift in emphasis away from resettlement and toward protection in the region.

### End Notes

[1] http://www.cis.org/rush/hearing-syrian-refugees-reassurance-and-storytelling.

[2] http://www.defenseone.com/management/2015/10/chattanoogas-wake-dhs-wants-revive-terrorism-alertsystem/122748/.

[3] http://cis.org/cadman/why-syrian-refugee-vetting-will-be-indisputably-fallible.

[4] "A separate world", The Buffalo News, September 23, 2002.

[5] http://www.washingtontimes.com/news/2015/feb/24/islamist-terror-groups-target-minnesota-somaliref/?page=all.

[6] http://www.usatoday.com/story/news/politics/2015/10/23/fbi-comey-isil-domestic-probes/ 74455460/.

[7] http://cis.org/911-HowMilitantIslamicTerroristsEntered.

[8] http://abcnews.go.com/Blotter/al-qaeda-kentucky-us-dozens-terrorists-country-refugees/story?id=20931131.

[9] http://www.nydailynews.com/news/crime/idaho-jury-convicts-uzbek-refugee-terror-charges-article-1.2323902.

[10] http://news.yahoo.com/bosnians-reject-hatred-wake-terror-financing-case-060550317.html.

[11] http://cis.org/High-Cost-of-Resettling-Middle-Eastern-Refugees.

[12] http://www.unhcr.org/pages/4f9016576.html.

# INDEX

## G



## H



## I



## J



## L



## M

## W